SACRED SITES OF WISCONSIN

JOHN-BRIAN PAPROCK
TERESA PENEGUY PAPROCK

Trails Books
Black Earth, Wisconsin

Library of Congress Control Number: 2001090810
ISBN: 1-931599-01-7

Editor: Stan Stoga
Photos: John-Brian Paprock
Design: Kortney Kaiser
Cover Design: John Huston
Cover Photo: Michael Shedlock
Back Cover Photo: Jason Koehl

Printed in the United States of America.
06 05 04 03 02 01   6 5 4 3 2 1

Trails Books, a division of Trails Media Group, Inc.
P.O. Box 317 • Black Earth, WI 53515
(800) 236-8088 • e-mail: books@wistrails.com
www.trailsbooks.com

Dedication

To our mothers, who encourage all our projects

Theotokos (Mother of God)

Gaeia (Mother Earth)

Wilma Mattingly (Teresa's mom)

And, especially,

Miriam Nancy Jean Summers, 1940-2000
(John-Brian's mom)

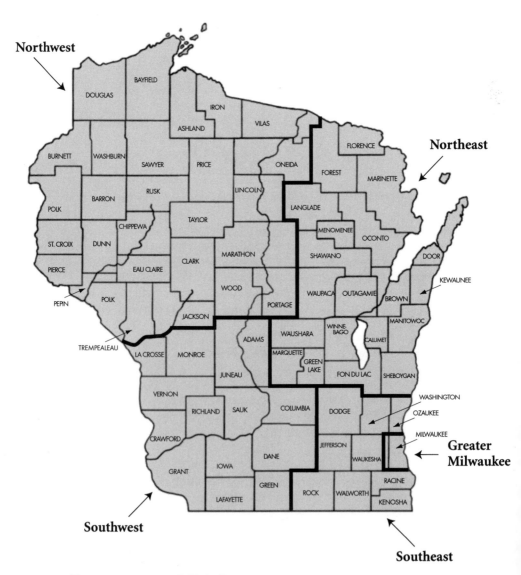

Northwest

Northeast

Southwest

Southeast

Greater Milwaukee

Regions of Wisconsin

Contents

1 Greater Milwaukee

2 Southeast Wisconsin

Lists of Sites by Religious Category

Preface

*A*ncient sites beckon you to hit the road soon.
—Message in a fortune cookie received by the authors before traveling
more than 9,000 miles to visit the sites for this book

Where Does One Find the Sacred?

People have always sought out those special places that seem to have a strong connection with the divine. The ancient Celts referred to them as "thin places," where the veil separating Earth from the spirit world was virtually transparent. They are the places that inspire feelings of awe, of reverence, of reassurance.

Throughout history, certain geographical spaces have attracted people of a particular religion or belief system—sometimes, more than one. Jews, Christians, and Moslems, for example, all claim Jerusalem as a sacred city. Early Christian churches were often built on land already considered sacred.

For the traveler seeking to find the spirit—however he or she chooses to define that term—Wisconsin provides countless opportunities. The state is home to hundreds of sacred sites, some well known and accessible, others hidden away and difficult to find. They include churches, temples, synagogues, cemeteries, effigy mounds, retreat centers, and more. We hope that *Sacred Sites of Wisconsin* will enlighten you about them and the beliefs and values they represent. The book provides the locations and descriptions of sacred spaces you may want to visit—either because they reflect your own belief system or they teach you about someone else's.

How Did We Get Started?

When we began to list the sacred sites for inclusion, we found no single resource for the information. We uncovered many instances of cultural or scientific selectivity and lots of confusing and contradictory data. We then started with an accumulated list of more than 850 sites in Wisconsin. It included some of the oldest holy places in the state, those that had meaning for ancient people, as well as being a source of inspiration for modern individuals. These sites transcend time and dogma to truly become "thin places." Because sacredness is outside of time, sites of great antiquity, as well as brand-new structures are included.

How Did We Choose These Sacred Places?

Because Wisconsin has so many sites considered sacred by various people, we had to choose the sites carefully for inclusion in this book. Generally, each sacred site described or listed has one or more of the following qualities:

- It is considered sacred by a group (or groups) of people, not an individual.
- It is on the National Register of Historic Places or is otherwise of historic significance. Properties on the National Register must be associated either with events of broad historical significance or with the lives of historically significant people; some other factors influencing the evaluation of these NRHP sites include distinctive architectural elements or high artistic value. We also included sites that were the subject of legends, a circumstance that made them culturally significant.
- It is otherwise unique. Some of the sites, for example, have national significance.

Then we rated the sites in four categories: historic relevance, uniqueness, aesthetic qualities, and intrinsic value (the "awe" factor). Those with the "best" scores were included in the book. Over 400 sites were chosen, although we wish we could have included more. Obviously, these are highly subjective categories, but the transcendent quality of these places needed a certain subjective, perhaps spiritual, response. The sites that ranked highest in each region were then named to our "Favorite Sites" listed at the beginning of each chapter. Although every site in this guide is well worth visiting, anyone interested in sacred sites should not miss our favorite ones.

What Can You Expect at the Sites?

Most of the sites can be visited for free or for a small admission charge. The public may view all of the sites listed here, with certain obvious limitations. Some are open all the time; others require advance arrangements (we've included phone numbers and contacts so you can call ahead). Some can be viewed only from the outside, usually because the sites are aging and in need of repair. We purposely did not include fragile or private places, unless the owners or protectors approved or insisted that we do so.

Various rules of conduct are appropriate for various sites. For example, some churches may require formal dress. Silence is appropriate at most sites, especially at Native American effigy mounds. It is inappropriate to picnic on the mounds. It is considered rude to walk on graves (including burial mounds). There are some other guidelines that the traveler should be aware of:

- When visiting a sacred site, especially if it represents a belief system different from your own, be cognizant of the reverence others have for it. Be respectful of others' beliefs about the location, even if you don't share those beliefs.

- Ask questions when appropriate. Take advantage of the visit to find out something you didn't know. But be respectful of people who may be at the site to worship. The site may be open only during worship periods. Take the time to stay and ask questions when worship is concluded.

- Ask about the appropriateness of taking photographs; although most public places do not have such restrictions, it is highly inappropriate to record certain ceremonies in any manner.

- It is always appropriate to pray or meditate quietly at any of these sites, but do not enter an altar area or touch sacred items without asking or being invited.

- Do not expect to be included in ceremonies or traditions to which you do not belong, and do not engage in ceremonies not approved by the current caretakers of the site. If there is any doubt, ask.

- Most important, these places have been considered, and must continue to be considered, holy places, sacred to at least one group of people, either at the present time or in the past. Ask yourself, "What makes this place sacred?" Can you "feel" its power?

May all your journeys and pilgrimages to sacred places be fruitful, nurturing, and healing. May the "thin places" bring you closer to things divine, allowing you to catch a glimpse of a world not normally seen.

Reverend John-Brian Paprock
Teresa Peneguy Paprock

Acknowledgments

We would like to thank God and all those who assisted in this endeavor:

Christopher River-Paprock, who spent much of the summer between second and third grades riding around with us to visit what he called our "secret sites."

Our parents—Wilma Mattingly, Ray Nielsen, Thomas Pigneguy, and the late Nancy "Miriam" Koehl—for their interest, encouragement, and support.

The hosts of the sites we visited, who honored us by welcoming us into their sacred spaces and taking the time to share their history and their faith with us.

The state agencies and local organizations that helped us compile the information we needed, no matter how obscure, especially the staff at the Wisconsin Historical Society.

Our friends and coworkers who supported us in countless ways, by providing suggestions, sharing ideas, and helping us stay optimistic even when the going got tough.

We debated about listing the names of many individuals who facilitated our visit to their sacred site and our adventure there. But we realized we might forget someone. So, to the many we wanted to remember (and those we did remember), please accept our deepest appreciation for all the information and assistance in our travels and pilgrimages.

God bless and keep each of you,
and may you be blessed tenfold the kindness you have shared.

Introduction

Religion in Wisconsin Sacred Places and Sacred Times

Our main business is not to see
what lies dimly at a distance,
but to do what lies clearly at hand.

—Thomas Carlyle

SOME OF THE FIRST INDICATIONS of humanity in the land that we have designated as Wisconsin go back at least 12,000 years. Recently, marks on mammoth bones found in Kenosha County show evidence of direct human contact. These have been dated so far back as to make Wisconsin one of three oldest sites of continual human existence in North America.

Ancient relics appear to have been related to the basic human needs for food, shelter, and religion. This should be no surprise. Religion is one of the central forces of all human culture. It is religion that interprets and integrates the cosmos, the awe-inspiring, the sacred. The timeless beauty of Wisconsin has awed people from numerous cultures across the centuries. Many places have become sacred over time, or perhaps they started in the sacred. These can be ceremonial and meditative locations used by several cultures. These can be places of tremendous natural or man-made beauty. These can be places of mystery or memorial. Designation of sacred space is a religious exercise that is both ancient and modern.

Little is known of the earliest cultures of Wisconsin. However, the Menominee people have stories of their emergence from a sacred stone place in northeastern Wisconsin. The enigmatic Copper Culture of northern Wisconsin is one of the least understood, and its sacred places have disappeared or become the sacred sites for another people's ceremony.

The earthen temple mounds and unusual burials of Aztalan pose their own set of enigmas. Were these built by the same mound builders that were so industrious throughout the region? Probably not. The effigy mound builders built different shapes and seemed particularly fond of places of tremendous natural beauty overlooking lakes or rivers. Were these effigy mound builders the ancestors of any current people living in Wisconsin? Yes, the Ho-Chunk Nation has legends and stories of their ancestors building the effigies along with other tribes and peoples. Each tribe, each culture, has a unique belief system, its own religion. Religious and spiritual people of other times would end up using some of the effigy mounds for their own purposes.

In 1634, about the time Roman Catholic settlements were developing in Maryland on the East Coast, the Huron people took Father Jean Nicolet and his French Catholic companions to meet the Ho-Chunk, the Menominee, and the Dakota peoples—the residents of this fair land. The French set up camps and chapels, the beginnings of towns and cities along the Great Lakes and major rivers. Some have become the major urban centers of Wisconsin.

During the remainder of the 17th century, Wisconsin saw mainly Native American immigrations from at least six different tribal affiliations, all being pushed north and west by the advancement of mostly white settlers. These immigrants also considered Wisconsin sacred land, honoring the ceremonial grounds throughout the land. Of course, there were tribal conflicts, and several places have become sacred because of the losses suffered or the peace gained there.

It wasn't until the 1800s that other European settlers began to establish communities, integrating the land with their distant cultures. Aside from a few Anglicans, most other non-Catholic Christians did not build their own chapels or churches until the 1840s. That is when the Lutheran communities began in southern Wisconsin, especially in the lead mining districts of what is now Grant County and the fertile farmland of Dane and Green Counties.

By 1900, settlers from at least 40 countries speckled Wisconsin, not including "free" black men and women. The concentrations were in the eastern and the southern regions of the state. Of course, there were ethnic Catholics (mostly German and Polish); there were also Lutherans and Methodists from Scandinavian countries. Slavic populations in the northern part of the state built Russian Orthodox Churches at the turn of the 20th century, and the Jewish communities in the industrial region of the Lake Michigan shores built synagogues in at least four metropolitan areas.

By the beginning of the past century, Wisconsin had already developed a reputation for experimentation. Humanistic and holistic worldviews found their homes here along with various schismatic groups. Christian Science, various sects of Mormonism, Spiritualists, and the Gideon's Bible Movement all have claim to their beginnings or early development here. Unitarians and

Universalists (which merged in 1961) had communities in southeastern and south-central cities. Several conservative schisms also found homes in this state, most notably the Wisconsin Evangelical Lutheran Synod.

Through the first half of the 20th century, population growth continued, mostly along the trodden paths of urban centers established by trade and commerce, but there were no significant changes in the religious demographics of the state until the 1960s. The 1960s brought new cultures to Wisconsin and new beginnings. Several ecumenical mergers of national churches created the United Church of Christ, the Unitarian Universalist Association, and the United Methodist Churches, as well as some unions among the various Lutheran groups. Perhaps the largest change in cultural and religious diversity came from the changes in the immigration laws that allowed larger numbers of immigrants from the Middle East and Asia. The oldest Muslim Student Organization in the United States was established at the University of Wisconsin-Madison in 1960.

This pluralistic growth continued in the 1970s. During this decade, Wisconsin offered refuge to exiled Cubans. Buddhism began to take root, the earliest Buddhist temples in the state date to the early 1970s. So do the first Middle East-style mosques. These have usually been renovated businesses and homes. The first federally recognized Wiccan "church" was organized in southwestern Wisconsin amid the very same sacred land of long-ago tribes that etched on the rocks and built the effigies.

In 1981, the Freedom from Religion Foundation was established in Madison, which had been known as a center for "freethinkers" for at least two generations.

It was during the 1980s that immigration of South Asians developed Hindu and Sikh societies in the major urban centers of Wisconsin. Also in the 1980s, Wisconsin opened its arms again to refugees, this time to Southeast Asians fleeing the persecution of the Khmer Rouge.

At the start of the 21st century, those of European Christian heritages are the majority of the population of Wisconsin. About 65 percent call themselves Christian. About 35 percent are Catholic, 26 percent are Lutheran, and there are fewer than 7 percent each of any other faith or denomination (nonreligious, atheist, and agnostic combined are about 7 percent statewide). The top five religions are Christianity, Judaism, Buddhism, Unitarian Universalism, and Islam. Although there are more than one million Native Americans in Wisconsin, there is a great diversity of cultural mores and religious beliefs among them. About 75 percent of Wisconsin's Native Americans are residents of northern Wisconsin. Those remaining are split almost evenly between Milwaukee and the rest of the state.

Reflective of the history of God's Country (as Wisconsin has been so nobly called) and the diversity of its people, the sacred sites of Wisconsin are both ancient and modern. Indeed, they are as timeless as the natural beauty that surrounds them.

Greater Milwaukee
Milwaukee County and eastern portion of Waukesha County.

Chapter 1

Greater
Milwaukee

*T*he perfect temple should stand at the center of the world;
a microcosm of the universe fabric, its walls built four
square with the walls of heaven.
—William Lethaby, *Architecture Mysticism and Myth*

IN A SOCIETY WHERE attendance at many traditional churches is dropping, Milwaukee has a large number of churches per capita, many churches have multiple services, and pews are full.

Milwaukee's rich ethnic heritage is reflected by its wide array of sacred sites and places of worship. On land believed to be sacred from the earliest days (native settlements within the city date back to 700 to 1300 C.E., today's Milwaukee reflects the amazing diversity of immigrants that hit the city in waves between the 18th and 20th centuries.

The Jesuits, who came during the late 1600s, were among the first white visitors to Milwaukee. Although Catholics now make up almost half of the one million residents of the Greater Milwaukee area, other faiths are well represented and have been since the city's beginnings. German Lutherans were among the first residents of the city, coming in the 1830s with the earliest wave of permanent white settlers.

The first Jewish worship service took place in 1850. Later, immigrants from Asia and the Middle East became numerous enough to form religious communities—Buddhist, Islamic, Sikh.

"Greater Milwaukee" can be defined in different ways. For the purposes of this guide, we are considering it to be Milwaukee County and the easternmost cities of Waukesha County.

*F*avorite Sites

- All Saints Episcopal Cathedral, downtown Milwaukee
  (the first Episcopal cathedral in the U.S.)

- Archdiocesan Marian Shrine, west side of Milwaukee
  (a peaceful place in the city)

- Eman-El B'Ne Jeshurun Congregation (synagogue), north side of
  Milwaukee (the largest synagogue building in the state)

- Gesu Parish Church, downtown Milwaukee
  (beautiful shrine chapels downstairs)

- Immanuel Presbyterian Church, downtown Milwaukee
  (a Protestant gem)

- Old St. Mary Church, downtown Milwaukee
  (oldest church in Milwaukee)

- Painesville Memorial Chapel (Frei Gemeinde), Franklin
  (first free Christian church in Wisconsin)

- Sacred Heart Roman Catholic Shrine and Seminary, Hales Corners
  (a concentric circle chapel)

- Sikh Religious Society of Wisconsin (gudwara), Brookfield
  (Wisconsin's first Sikh gudwara)

- St. Joan of Arc Chapel, downtown Milwaukee
  (authentic medieval chapel)

- Basilica of St. Josephat, south side of Milwaukee
  (breathtakingly beautiful)

- St. Mark African Methodist Episcopal Church, north side of Milwaukee
  (shaped like an anvil)

- St. Sava Serbian Orthodox Cathedral, south side of Milwaukee
  (interior entirely covered in Italian mosaic)

- St. Stephen Catholic Church, south side of Milwaukee
  (the "airport church," with beautiful wood carvings)

The triple spires of Trinity Evangelical Lutheran Church, Milwaukee

Catholic Sites

Pere Marquette Park

Pere Marquette Park is named for missionary and explorer Father Jacques Marquette, who camped at this site in 1674 and was visited by nearby Indians. The Jesuit priest is the first recorded white explorer to the area and was said to have been deeply respected by the Native Americans.

According to custom, Father Marquette would have blessed the camp where he was staying and celebrated Mass there, making the park the first Catholic sacred place in the area. A gazebo marker by the river marks the place where Marquette is said to have stayed.

Located at 910 N. Old World Third Street
(at the corner of Kilbourn Avenue), (414) 273-8288.
milwaukee-naturally.com/placestogo/peremarquette.htm

St. Joan of Arc Chapel

Even many Milwaukeeans don't realize their city boasts the oldest continuous-use structure in the Western Hemisphere. Built during the 1400s (before the birth of Christopher Columbus) this small Gothic chapel, originally named Chapelle de St. Martin de Sayssuel, was the ecclesiastical center of the village of Chasse, France. Today it stands in the center of the Marquette University campus in downtown Milwaukee.

The stone chapel, deteriorating after the French revolution, was discovered by architect and archeologist Jacques Couelle. He made architectural drawings and took photographs and measurements during the 1920s. He negotiated the dismantling and transfer, brick-by-brick, to Long Island, New York, in 1926 after the chapel was purchased by an American. At this time the famous Joan of Arc stone was added (more on this below).

The chapel became the property of Marquette University in 1964 and was dismantled and shipped brick-by-brick again, this time to Milwaukee. At that time it was dedicated to St. Joan of Arc. Visiting the chapel is the only opportunity for tourists to enjoy the experience of walking into a medieval structure while remaining on American soil. Visitors can also see a crucifix, torchères, candlesticks, lectern, and vestments from the period of the chapel. The chapel's most curious feature is the Joan of Arc stone, which has remained several degrees colder than the stones around it since Joan of Arc kissed the stone before she was martyred in 1431—an unexplained phenomenon.

The chapel is open for tours daily from 10 a.m. to 4 p.m. and closed on all major holidays. Regular services are held. Admission is free.

*Located directly behind the Marquette Memorial
Library, 1415 W. Wisconsin Avenue (between
Clybourn and Wisconsin Avenues), (414) 288-6873.
cin.org/churches/joanarc.html*

Old St. Mary Catholic Church

Built in 1846, Old St. Mary Church is the oldest church of any denomination still standing in Milwaukee. The start of its construction was simultaneous with Milwaukee's official birth as a city. Milwaukee's earliest German immigrants built the church with help from Bavarian mission societies. King Ludwig I of Bavaria presented the painting of the Annunciation as a gift in 1848; it still hangs over the altar. The church interior was restored by Conrad Schmitt Studios in 1982.

A comparatively plain black, Cream City brick exterior gives little hint of the splendor to be found inside. The church continues to serve a vibrant congregation, and the St. Anne Women's Society (founded in 1844) is still active today. A church pamphlet refers to the church's City of Milwaukee Landmark status and its listing in the National Register of Historic Places, but adds, "Important as these honors are, its greatest service remains in the spiritual harvest of souls . . . There is an intangible magnetism about this venerable, special church, a certain indescribable attraction in its old-world atmosphere."

St. Mary is open from 6 to 9 a.m. each day for Mass, and again from 11 a.m.

to 1 p.m., with Mass at 12:05 p.m. Group tours are available on request by appointment, and visitors are welcome to attend at any time.

Located at 844 N. Broadway (corner of Kilbourn Avenue), across from the City Hall Annex, (414) 271-6180. www.oldstmarys.org/introduction/intro.html

Old St. Mary Catholic Church, Milwaukee

Basilica of St. Josephat

Constructed between 1897 and 1901, the Basilica of St. Josephat was the first basilica in the United States and is the only Polish basilica in North America. It features one of the top-five largest domes in the world—at 200 feet high, it's amazing from the outside and absolutely breathtaking from within. St. Josephat's is incomparable, a must-see for anyone with an appreciation for sacred beauty.

The largest church in Milwaukee, St. Josephat's seats 2,400. It was built from 200,000 tons of stonework rescued from Chicago's Federal Building, which had been demolished in 1895. Much of the labor was performed by the church's own parishioners. The parish, which began with a small number of poor Polish immigrants, would become one of eight large Polish parishes in the city during the early 1900s.

St. Josephat's glowing clock is a familiar sight around Milwaukee's South Side. The church building houses a congregation and serves as a locale for musical events due to its amazing acoustics. Those who visit the basilica will see the end results of many changes over the century. Roman artist Professor

Gonippo Raggi designed the ornate interior decor in 1926, which includes marbleized columns, rag-rolled walls, and 65 murals. The decor was simplified in 1965 according to guidelines of Vatican II. Then the basilica was restored to its original decorative scheme in 1996, including conservation of the 1902 Innsbruck stained glass windows.

The basilica has an estimated 27,000 visitors each year. A visitor center opened in the summer of 2000 features a gift shop, donor's chapel, and handicapped facilities. Visitors can call for tour information. Regular services are held.

Located at 601 W. Lincoln Avenue
(corner of South Sixth Street),
(414) 645-5623. thebasilica.org

Archdiocesan Marian Shrine

This little park, nestled in a humble residential area on Milwaukee's west side, is a true sanctuary for the soul. Open to the public, the park features a Lourdes grotto with an impressive collection of religious statues, an altar in a locked enclosure, and the Stations of the Cross in bass relief. Rosary beads, prayer cards, and booklets are available at the site. The shrine was founded in 1947 after World War II and rededicated in 1976 to the Immaculate Heart of Mary.

Located at 141 N. 68th Street,
(414) 257-0155. More information is
available from the Archdiocesan office, (414) 769-3300.
fcsn.k12.nd.us/Shanley.broanth/marianshrine.htm.

Gesu Parish Church

Located in downtown Milwaukee, near the Marquette University campus, Gesu Parish was built in 1893. It features a striking cathedral-style sanctuary upstairs and a cozy chapel downstairs with a series of devotional shrines dedicated to various saints. The congregation is the result of the 1894 a merger between St. Gall's and Holy Name, two Irish parishes serving what was known as Tory Hill. Daily Masses are held Monday though Friday almost hourly, and four Masses are offered on Sundays. This is part of our Downtown Milwaukee Church Walk (see page 10).

Located at 1145 W. Wisconsin Avenue, just north
of Marquette University, (414) 288-7101.
marquette.edu/places/gesu.html; www.execpc.com/gesupar

Holy Trinity (Our Lady of Guadalupe) Roman Catholic Church

A German Zopfstil-style building erected in 1849-1850, Holy Trinity is one of Milwaukee's oldest churches. Its architect, Victor Schulte, also designed St. Mary and St. John's churches. This building was designated a City of Milwaukee Landmark in 1970. Holy Trinity School, next door, was built in 1867 and is the oldest school building in the city of Milwaukee. The building is on the list of the National Register of Historic Places. Masses are said in English and Spanish, and the parish is a major resource for Milwaukee's Hispanic community. Regular services are held.

Located at 605–613 S. Fourth Street, (414) 271-6181.

Risen Savior Shrine, Church of St. Jude the Apostle

A small shrine in a pyramidal grotto was dedicated in 1990 on the south side of St. Jude's Catholic Church. During the summer, the shrine is covered in flowers. Surrounding prayer benches make this a place for reflection and meditation.

Located at 734 Glenview Avenue, Wauwatosa,
(414) 258-8821.

Sacred Heart School of Theology and Shrine

Just off of Highway 100 south of Milwaukee, the Sacred Heart complex offers a serene garden shrine and monastery that can be toured; a gift shop; and concerts.

The facility was dedicated by the Priests of the Sacred Heart of Jesus in 1929. The name was changed to Sacred Heart Monastery in 1932, when it became the home of the seminary program of the Priest of the Sacred Heart in the United States. The college program relocated to Loyola University (Chicago) in the mid-1950s. The name changed to Sacred Heart School of Theology in 1968, when the new facility was built.

The chapel features a unique concentric circle design with the altar in the middle, a design made possible due to changes with Vatican II. The unique crown and cross atop the building can be seen from a distance. Regular services are held.

Located at 7335 Lovers Lane Road (South Highway 100), southwest
of Milwaukee. From I-894/43, get off at the Hales Corners exit and
take Highway 100 approximately three miles south, (414) 529-6966.

St. George Syrian Catholic Church

St. George Syrian Catholic Church is an Eastern Rite Catholic church—under

Rome, but in many ways quite similar to Eastern Orthodox churches. The building reflects old-world design patterns, with three sheet-metal onion domes, which, according to the church Web site, "allude to that which is above and beyond the harshness of this earth."

Completed in 1917, the St. George Syrian Catholic Church (also called St. George Melkite Greek Catholic Church) was designed by Erhard Brielmaier and Sons (they also designed the Basilica of St. Josephat and St. Benedict the Moor; see separate listings). The interior contains the kind of elaborate iconography found in Eastern Orthodox churches. It is listed on the National Register of Historic Places and has been referenced in several publications and included in the city of Milwaukee's Ethnic Church Tour. Regular services are held.

Located at 1617 W. State Street, (414) 342-1543.
dsha.k12.wi.us/Melkite/Georgehome.htm

St. Francis Seminary and Marian Center

Located on Lake Michigan with an awesome southern view of the Milwaukee skyline, the St. Francis Seminary and Marian Center provides a number of items of interest to the visitor including a hermitage, the Perpetual Adoration Chapel, the Marian Center (formerly St. Mary's Academy), and the Grape Arbor walk.

The seminary was founded in 1856 (named after St. Francis de Sales), while the academy was founded 10 years later. The complex includes a convent and retirement center for nuns. A variety of architectural styles exist on the property, along with grottos attributed to Fr. Paul Dobberstein and numerous religious statues.

Part of the facility, the St. Joseph House of Prayer is offered as a retreat center; for a small donation, it provides overnight lodging, meals, a daily liturgy, and spiritual direction. The RIETI Hermitage, on the same grounds, also provides lodging, access to the convent library, daily liturgy, and services of a spiritual director, all for a small donation. According to the literature, RIETI "is based on the belief of our oneness with all creation, of our need for community in solitude, and of a sense of mission."

Located at 3221–3257 S. Lake Drive, St. Francis (south side of Milwaukee).
Visitors are asked to call first: St Francis Seminary, (414) 747-6400;
Marian Center, (414) 744-4146 or (414) 744-1160.
Archbishop Cousins Archdiocesan Retreat Center is
located just south at 3501 S. Lake Drive, (414) 769-3491. lakeosfs.org

St. Stephen Catholic Church

For its sheer determination to survive, St. Stephen Catholic Church deserves note. But "the little parish at the airport," as it calls itself, also has some of the most ornate European Gothic-style woodcarvings and architecture to be found in the Midwest.

Founded in 1847 by German settlers, St. Stephen's church buildings were destroyed by fire in 1908 and again in 1927. The second fire left only the 139-foot bell tower and four walls standing. Next, the building, located on south Howell Avenue, happened to be smack in the middle of expansion plans for General Mitchell International Airport. "It is recorded that the pilots themselves even requested the church remain where it was, for the bell tower served as a landmark when approaching the runways," according to church literature. Eventually it was decided that the airport would build around the church. It was declared a City of Milwaukee Landmark in 1980.

Visitors to St. Stephen will be keenly aware of airplanes zooming closely overhead, and they'll also notice that parishioners pay no mind. The church is worth a visit to see the exquisite woodwork inside. Guided tours are available by appointment. Regular services are held.

Located at 5880 S. Howell Avenue (south of Layton Avenue between Grange and College Avenues, adjacent to General Mitchell International Airport), (414) 483-2685.

Cathedral of St. John the Evangelist

Built in 1847 and on the National Register of Historic Places, the congregation was formerly St. Peter's, which was founded in 1839. It was one of the first English-speaking parishes in Milwaukee. The entrance is adorned with an eagle, the symbol of St. John. There is an extraordinary tabernacle inside. Many consider this cathedral to be one of the most sacred places in Milwaukee. Regular services are held.

Located at 802 N. Jackson Street (at State Street, adjacent to Jackson Park), (414) 276-9814.

St. Benedict the Moor Catholic Church

A predominantly African-American congregation, "St. Ben's" has a special mission for social justice and "those who have felt rejected and excluded elsewhere." It was built in 1923, designed by Erhard Brielmaier and Sons. Sunday liturgy at 10 a.m.

Located at 1015 N. Ninth Street, (414) 271-0135.

A Downtown Milwaukee Church Walk

With a short, half-hour walk, visitors to downtown Milwaukee can easily see several churches with historic and spiritual significance and vastly different architectural styles. For a quick tour, we suggest parking at 10th Street and Tory Hill (just east of the Marquette University campus) on the southwest side of downtown. Downtown Milwaukee is mapped out on a grid system and is fairly easy to navigate. Then, check out the following:

St. James Epsicopal Church, *833 W. Wisconsin Avenue, across from the Milwaukee Public Library. (See page 12.)*

Calvary Presbyterian Church, *935 W. Wisconsin Avenue, at the corner of 10th Street. (See page 14.)*

Gesu Parish Church (Catholic), *1145 W. Wisconsin Avenue. (See page 6.)*

St. Joan of Arc Chapel (medieval-era Catholic), *behind Marquette Memorial Library at 1415 W. Wisconsin Avenue. (See page 3.)*

Episcopal Sites
All Saints Episcopal Cathedral Complex

The first Episcopal cathedral in the United States, All Saints Episcopal was built in 1866, under the authority of Bishop Jackson Kemper, and designed by Edward Townsend Mix. The cathedral features a beautiful triptych (three-panel picture) in the main sanctuary. The recently renovated Holy Family Chapel is part of the Bishop Nichol's House that contains the diocesan offices. The chapel was built almost 50 years ago to accommodate the wheelchair-bound wife of a former diocesan bishop. Several times a week, the chapel has prayer services at noon. The current bishop's residence and administrative offices are part of the yellow brick complex and are next to the church where regular Sunday services are held. A garden graces the area in between. Regular services are held.

Located at E. 804–828 Juneau Avenue, north of downtown Milwaukee, (414) 271-7719. ascathedral.org/CathedralTour.html

St. Paul's Episcopal Church

Organized in 1836, St. Paul's is Wisconsin's third oldest Episcopal parish, and the oldest in Milwaukee. St. Paul's congregation developed and managed the Forest Home Cemetery (see below). The Richardsonian Romaneque church building, built in 1890, is made of striking dark red sandstone and features a massive bell tower surrounded by larger-than-life-sized angel sculptures. The Tiffany Studios in New York furnished "Christ Leaving the Praetorium," the largest Tiffany window ever made. Parts of the glass are more than two inches thick. Regular services are held.

Located at 904 E. Knapp Street north of downtown Milwaukee, (414) 276-6277. stpaulsmilwaukee.org

Detailed stonework of St. Paul's Episcopal Church

Forest Home Cemetery and Chapel

Almost 200 acres, Forest Home Cemetery was developed by members of St. Paul's Episcopal Church in the 1840s, back when the property was far away from urban hustle and bustle. The cemetery, which was founded after an epidemic of ship's fever claimed many lives in Milwaukee, features a large-stoned English Gothic Episcopal chapel flanked by greenhouses that run alongside the pews, one of the first outdoor garden mausoleums in the United States, and the Halls of History Museum. It's now a nonprofit organization serving people of all faiths.

2405 W. Forest Home Avenue (at Lincoln), (414) 645-2632.

St. James Episcopal Church

This Gothic Revival building was built in 1867 but was rebuilt after a devastating fire in 1872. It has a breathtaking cathedral-size nave and a beautiful wood-carved altar. The congregation dates back to 1851. Regular services are held. It is part of our Downtown Milwaukee Church Walk (see page 10).

Located at 833 W. Wisconsin Avenue, near the Marquette University campus, (414) 271-1340.

Eastern Orthodox Sites

Annunciation Greek Orthodox Church

Certainly one of Milwaukee's most famous sights, and perhaps the best-known Eastern Orthodox church building in the United States, the circular Annunciation Greek Orthodox Church was Frank Lloyd Wright's last major project.

Completed in 1961, the building features a blue-tiled dome roof 106 feet in diameter. Byzantine design dictates a dome over the center area of a cross-shaped building; Wright's design departed from the usual Greek Orthodox practice by placing the dome over the entire building. The original congregation was one of the 10 oldest Greek Orthodox congregations in the United States.

While the building's design has been both celebrated and criticized, the congregation has been thankful for its many tourists over the years and considers the building a way to promote awareness of a faith that is unfamiliar to many. It's said to have "put Orthodoxy on the map." Tours are available after services on Sunday, but it's recommended that you call first and dress fairly formally to be respectful. As with most Frank Lloyd Wright buildings, the exterior is a spectacular sight. Matins at 8:30 a.m. and liturgy at 9:30 a.m. on Sunday.

Located at 9400 W. Congress Street, Wauwatosa, Milwaukee County, (414) 461-9400. wrightinwisconsin.org/WisconsinSites/Annunciation/

St. Sava Serbian Orthodox Cathedral

St. Sava's congregation formed in 1912 and built the current church building in 1958-59. It is the only Serbian Orthodox cathedral in Wisconsin. The church features a central dome and four corner domes, but the real treasure is inside. The walls and ceiling are lavishly covered with iconography made of Italian mosaic, copies of mosaics from Serbian medieval monasteries. It's one of only a tiny handful of churches around the world decorated exclusively with mosaic. Large, beautiful chandeliers on either side of the nave are surrounded by traditional icons that are lit from behind. The church contains many examples of the artwork unique to Eastern Orthodox houses of worship.

The large congregation reflects immigration that came in several waves—first for economic and then for political reasons. Many refugees now attend the church, which serves Serbian Orthodox from as far away as Madison and Chicago. Services are held in English and Serbian. Call ahead for information on touring the premises.

Located at 3201 S. 51st Street, (414) 545-4080.

The Domes of St. Sava Serbian Orthodox Cathedral, Milwaukee

St. John the Baptist Armenian Apostolic Church & Holy Resurrection Armenian Apostolic Church

Both small mission churches, St. John the Baptist and Holy Resurrection hold services every other Sunday, with the priest alternating between the two. Holy Resurrection's church building was built in 1961. St. John the Baptist has a building of modern design built in 1985.

St. John features a glorious series of stained glass windows with scenes of the nativity, crucifixion, resurrection, and ascension, designed by a Milwaukee Armenian artist. Services are held in English and Armenian. (See chapter 5 for the other Armenian Orthodox churches in Wisconsin.)

St. John is located at 7825 W. Layton Avenue in Greenfield, (414) 282-1670.
Holy Resurrection is located at 909 Michigan Avenue
in South Milwaukee, (414) 762-7460.

Presbyterian Sites

Immanuel Presbyterian Church

An awesome beauty of a church, Immanuel is another Edward Townsend Mix creation. Designed in 1873 in the Victorian Gothic style with extraordinary stained glass images, its builders used buff-colored and rock-faced limestone, along with gray and red sandstone. One of the towers is 147 feet high. The church advertises that its congregation has been "Growing with Milwaukee since 1837." Regular services are held at 10 a.m. Sundays.

Located at 1100 N. Astor Street, (414) 276-4757.

Immanuel Presbyterian Church, Milwaukee

Calvary Presbyterian Church

Calvary Presbyterian is constructed of Milwaukee's own Cream City brick, but it has been painted red. Instead of a cross, there is a poppy-head finial at the top of the steeple. Calvary has a labyrinth (see page 177) and is part of our Downtown Milwaukee Church Walk (page 10). Regular services are held.

Located at 935 W. Wisconsin Avenue, just east of the Marquette University campus, (414) 271-8782.

Other Christian Sites

St. Mark African Methodist Episcopal Church

The symbol of the African Methodist Episcopal (AME) church is the anvil—

because the denomination started in a blacksmith shop in Philadelphia by African-Americans who left a racist church, and because an anvil is strong. St. Mark's church building is shaped like an anvil and uses anvil imagery throughout.

Located near the Rufus King neighborhood on the city's north side, St. Mark's enriches its community with a wide variety of activities such as basketball and tutoring. It works along with the Milwaukee Public Schools to provide programs through its Quality of Life center.

The congregation began meeting in 1868 downtown at Wisconsin Avenue and Plankinton. The original building was located at Fourth and Cedar (now Fourth and Kilbourn), currently the site of the Hyatt Regency. A historical marker is located there; St. Mark's was the first African-American organization in Wisconsin to be awarded a historical marker. Erected in 1869, the original building was the first African-American church building in Wisconsin. The current anvil-shaped building was built in 1969. Regular services are held.

Located at 1616 W. Atkinson Avenue, (414) 562-8030.

The symbolic anvil at St. Mark AME Church, Milwaukee

Freewill Baptist Church

No longer in operation as a church, Freewill Baptist church is part of the Prospect Hill Settlement Historic District. It was occupied from 1859 (when it was in the "nucleus of the Yankee settlement") until 1925. Destroyed by arson in 1985, it was rebuilt in 1990. Across from the building is a breathtaking view of the valley with Little Muskego Lake.

Located at 19750 W. National (at the corner of Racine)
in New Berlin, Waukesha County, (262) 679-3448.

Freewill Baptist Church, New Berlin

Trinity Evangelical Lutheran Church-Missouri Synod

This is Milwaukee's oldest Lutheran church and the state of Wisconsin's oldest Missouri Synod church, dating back to 1878. Beautiful triple spires, which symbolize the Trinity (Father, Son, and Holy Spirit), reach toward the sky beside I-43. Regular services are held.

Located at 1046 N. Ninth Street
(at West Highland), (414) 271-2219.

Fox Point Burying Ground— Reformed Church of Bethlehem

Adjacent to Doctors Park in the prosperous suburb of Fox Point, the site formerly contained a log schoolhouse that housed the Reformed Church of Bethlehem, part of the Dutch Reformed movement. The building is gone, although it's easy to visualize where it may have been; a fence prevents entry to a cemetery, now called the Fox Point Burying Ground, with grave markers dating back to 1854. There is a beautiful view of Lake Michigan from here. The park is just south of the Schlitz Audubon Center.

Located just south of Doctors Park, which is at
1870 E. Fox Lane Road, Bayside/Fox Point.

Painesville Memorial Chapel (Freethinkers)

Also known as Freie Germeinde, the Painesville Chapel was the first Free Christian church in Wisconsin, located in the town of Franklin. It was erected in 1851 and is on the National Register of Historic Places. The building was built by Protestants from Wittenburg, Germany. It is believed that it was used by the Underground Railroad during the Civil War.

These "Freethinkers" were theologically closer to liberal Christians or Unitarian Universalists than to the agnostics or atheists commonly referred to as Freethinkers today. The building is currently vacant. Chapter 5 contains the listing of the Sauk City Freethinkers Hall, now being used by a Unitarian Universalist Congregation.

Located at 2740 W. Ryan Road and 27th Street, Franklin, Milwaukee County.

Buddhist Sites

Phuoc-Hou Buddhist Temple of Milwaukee

The only thing on the outside that identifies this former office building as a Buddhist temple is a golden Buddha gazing out of the window above the door, but the building contains an elaborate Vietnamese Buddhist altar. It is used by multiple Buddhist groups, both ethnic and American. It serves 600 people with Sunday services for both children and adults, as well as other activities.

Located at 1575 W. Oklahoma Avenue, (414) 383- 1155. nyobzoo.com/lao_buddhist_temple.htm

Milwaukee Zen Center

This Center, affiliated with the Soto Zen School, was founded in the mid-1970s, making it one of the oldest continuously running Buddhist centers in Wisconsin. It's open for sittings Monday through Saturday mornings, 6 to 7:30 a.m., and Monday through Friday evenings, 6 to 8 p.m.

Located at 2825 N. Stowell Avenue, between Linnwood Avenue and Kenwood Boulevard, (414) 963-0526. students.depaul.edu/jfutrans/zen.html

Wat Pathonmaphoutharan (Lao Buddhist Temple)

This beautiful temple is tucked away, deep inside the old former Pythian Castle (a fraternal building built in 1927 and on the National Register of Historic Places). It's adjacent to Phan's Garden, which offers outstanding Chinese/Vietnamese Cuisine.

Located at 1925 W. National Avenue, (414) 342-2721.
dancris.com/byblos/watlao.htm

The minaret of Masjid al Iman, Milwaukee

*I*slamic *Sites*

Masjid al Iman—Islamic Society of Milwaukee

Founded by ethnic Muslims, this large cream-colored converted and expanded school building features a 50-foot minaret capped by a dome with a crescent moon on the top. A private school, Salam School, shares the facility.

The center is owned by the North American Islamic Trust and is operated by the Islamic Society of Milwaukee, the largest Islamic organization in Wisconsin. The facility features a 70-by-70-foot prayer hall, Masjid Al Iman, with a balcony area for women. The hall holds about 500 men and 250 women. The building has one main entrance, but most women use the west entrance at the rear of the building instead of the main entrance. The center is open for five daily prayers.

Tours of the building, with information on Islam, are held during regular business hours and can be arranged by calling in advance.

Located at 4707 S. 13th Street (at Layton Avenue), on Milwaukee's south side, (414) 282-1812. marquette.edu/servicelearning/sites/islamic.html

Muhammad Mosque #3

Organized in 1940, this Nation of Islam mosque was the first mosque of any kind in the state of Wisconsin and the third Nation of Islam mosque in the nation (after Mosque #1, in Detroit, and Mosque #2, in Chicago). Elijah Muhammad, founder of the Nation of Islam (American Black Muslim Movement), formed a study group in Milwaukee in 1935. The mosque was located in several different locations before moving to its current location on Milwaukee's near north side. Other mosques and Muslim centers on Milwaukee's near north side are spin-off groups from the Nation of Islam.

Located at 4202 N. Teutonia Avenue (between Capitol Drive and Congress Street). Call ahead at (414) 444-7726 or (414) 406-1666.

Jewish Sites

Congregation Beth Israel

A Conservative Jewish synagogue, Beth Israel's congregation was founded in 1884 as Congregation B'ne Jacob. It was incorporated in 1886 by Moses Montefiore Gemeinde. By 1890, Milwaukee had a Jewish population of 7,000. A new synagogue was built on Fifth Street, and the building was sold in 1924.

The current building, in Glendale, had its first service in 1962. It includes a gift shop, library, museum, and a beautiful wooden chapel and Sephardim, which holds the Torah. The synagogue has office hours from 8:30 a.m. to 4:40 p.m., Monday through Thursday, and from 8:30 a.m. to noon on Friday.

Located at 6880 N. Green Bay Avenue Southeast, Glendale, (414) 352-7310. uscj.org/midwest/milwaukeecbi/top.html

Eman-El B'Ne Jeshurun Congregation, Milwaukee

Eman-El B'Ne Jeshurun Congregation

This Reform congregation, formed in 1856, has two campuses: one across from the University of Wisconsin–Milwaukee Student Union, and one on Milwaukee's far north side in the suburb of River Hills.

The original facility, known as the Kenwood campus, is a limestone neoclassical building built in 1922 with a majestic, theaterlike interior and an exhibit of menorahs, amulets, Passover plates, and documents from the 1800s. The Zilber Campus is a new and modern facility, recently erected. On display there is a Krystallnacht (literally, "night of breaking glass") Torah, rescued from the Holocaust era.

The first Jewish congregation in Milwaukee was established with the formation of the Emanu-El Cemetery Association in 1848. A group who wanted to adopt Polish liturgical customs broke away and formed Ahabath Emunah. In 1855, a group within that congregation split off to form Anshe Emeth, which followed German customs. Emanu-El and Ahabath Emunah then consolidated and formed B'ne Jeshurun.

Kenwood campus is located at 2419 E. Kenwood Boulevard, Milwaukee. Zilber Campus is located at 2020 Brown Deer Road in River Hills, (414) 228-7545.

Milwaukee– "The Gathering Place"

The Potawatomi Indians, living at what is now the mouth of the Milwaukee River, called the area the "Great Council Place" or *Mah-au-wauk-seepe:* "The Gathering Place by the River." It was a popular meeting place for those of different tribes. Because of its natural resources, the Ojibwes called the area *Man-na-wah-kie:* "The Good Land."

The tradition continues in such events as Indian Summer Days at the Milwaukee lakefront, an annual event in the fall. This huge gathering welcomes Native Americans from many nations for a weekend of music, food, crafts, and dance. One need not be Native American to participate in the powwow or prayer service. There's a village with traditional Native American dwellings like tepees, wooden lodges, and birch bark wigwams, and a re-created rustic trader encampment nearby. Information on dates, hours, and ticket prices is available from the Indian Summer Office, 7441 W. Greenfield Avenue, Suite 109, Milwaukee, WI 53214. For more information, phone (414) 774-7119; fax number is (414) 774-6810.

Native American Sites

Potawatomi Indian Village Site

There is only a marker to show where there was once an Indian village dating from approximately 500 C.E. This is now the site of the Hilton Hotel.

Plaque located at 509 W. Wisconsin Avenue, across from the Midwest Express Center.

Lake Park Mound

One of the few remaining effigy mounds in the Milwaukee area is located at Lake Park downtown. There is a low conical mound on the bluff overlooking Lake Michigan in the northeast corner of the park. The mound measures 40 feet in diameter.

Park entrance located at Kenwood Boulevard and Lake Drive.

Other Sites

Tripoli Shrine Temple Mosque

This ornate Shrine Temple dominates the skyline on West Wisconsin Avenue. Opened in May 1928, and entered into the National Register of Historic Places in 1986, the shrine is patterned after an Arabian castle with a 30-foot dome. It houses the Milwaukee chapter of the Ancient Arabic Order of the Nobles of the Mystic Shrine (the "Shriners"), a Masonic organization. Its purpose includes the operation of hospitals for children who need orthopedic and/or burn treatment. Although not a religion in its own right, it does require members to believe in God, and the organization is built on Judeo-Christian principles.

Located at 3000 W. Wisconsin Avenue, west of the Marquette University campus, (414) 933-4700. webruler.com/shriners/tripoli.htm

The tiled domes of Tripoli Shrine Temple Mosque, Milwaukee

Sikh Religious Society of Wisconsin Gudwara

This modern building, built by the Sikh Religious Society of Wisconsin, is the first Sikh gudwara (place of worship) in Wisconsin. The gudwara is set up for reading from scriptures and sharing of ceremonial meals. One sits on the floor in the gudwara. Smoking—even before visiting the temple—is strongly discouraged. Sunday services are held with prasad, a communal meal held after the teachings.

Sikhism, which originated in India, teaches a belief in one God as taught through 10 historical gurus, or teachers. Their teachings are preserved in the Adi Granth, or scriptures.

Located at 3675 N. Calhoun Road (south of Capitol Drive) in Brookfield, Waukesha County, (262) 790-1600. The only other gudwara in Wisconsin, the Gudwara Sahib, is in Middleton (near Madison) on Century Avenue.

Morris Pratt Institute

The Morris Pratt Institute is the seminary of the National Spiritualist Association; the oldest spiritualist organization in the United States, founded in Chicago in 1893.The Spiritualist movement has a long history in Wisconsin. (For more information, see chapter 3 and the Western Wisconsin Spiritual Center in chapter 5.)

Spiritualists believe in clairvoyance, prophecy, speaking in tongues, independent (or automatic) writing, and communication between the living and the dead. The movement enjoyed great popularity around the turn of the century. One Spiritualist church on Milwaukee's near north side advertises "healing and spiritual advice."

Located at 11811 Watertown Plank Road, Wauwatosa, (414) 774-2994. morrispratt.org

Southeast

Southeast Wisconsin

Including the counties of Dodge, Jefferson, Kenosha, Ozaukee, Racine, Rock, Walworth, Washington, and Waukesha

Chapter 2

Southeast Wisconsin

*I*n every life God raises up holy places
where He means us to find Him.

—Robert Runcie, *Archbishop of Canterbury*

HILLS SEEM TO invite worship of the divine. A hilltop provides a place that seems at once to be surrounded by the world and yet somehow separate from it. For those who understand the heavens to be "up there," a hilltop provides a way to be a bit closer to them. The hilly region of southeast Wisconsin is rich in sacred sites connected to hills and the lakes that often accompany them geographically.

The world-known Holy Hill overlooks the Kettle Moraine. With its Gothic Catholic church and lookout tower—and the miraculous tales of those who have been healed there—Holy Hill is a "must-see" for pilgrims regardless of faith.

Take a short journey to the south, and you discover the rolling Welsh Hills in Waukesha County, where there was once a collection of small Presbyterian churches built by immigrants. Some of the churches remain, and the entire area still seems to resonate from the singing festivals and other celebrations that were held there. Bryn Mawr (literally, "big hill") Road was named for one of the community's religious festivals.

A hill by the White River near Burlington had a different kind of significance for James Jesse Strang. Strang founded a large settlement of "Strangite Mormons" there at what he called the Hill of Promise in the mid-1800s. It was at this hill that Strang is said to have discovered three brass plates with spiritual writings on them.

Mounds are small man-made hills with a significance modern people can only guess at. The well-preserved Lizard Mound in Washington County, the platform mounds of Aztalan, and the world's only known intaglio (carved into the ground) are all found in southeast Wisconsin.

*F*avorite *Sites*

↩ **Aztalan Village State Park, Lake Mills**
(well-preserved temple mounds)

↩ **Cedar Valley Retreat Center, West Bend**
(cement and stained glass tepee)

↩ **DeKoven Center, Racine**
(rich in history)

↩ **Hindu Temple of Wisconsin, Pewaukee**
(Wisconsin's first Hindu temple)

↩ **Holy Hill National Shrine of Mary, Hubertus**
(can you make it to the top?)

↩ **Holy Trinity Episcopal Church, Waupun**
(Red and white Gothic revival design)

↩ **Jain Temple of Wisconsin, Pewaukee**
(unique in the state)

↩ **Lizard Mound County Park, West Bend**
(large group of unique and unusual effigy mounds)

↩ **Miracle, the White Buffalo, Janesville**
(a living prophecy)

↩ **Nashotah House Seminary Grounds, Delafield**
(beautiful and historic Chapel of St. Mary the Virgin)

↩ **The Recording Angel, Waupun**
(a beautiful and powerful sculpture in a peaceful setting)

↩ **Siena Center, Wind Point, Racine**
(40 serene acres on Lake Michigan)

↩ **St. Francis Retreat Center, Burlington**
(exquisite wood-carved chapel and wonderful grotto gardens)

↩ **St. John Chrysostom Church, Delafield**
(historic A-frame church next to St. John's Military Academy)

_9 **St. Mary's Roman Catholic Church, Port Washington**
(overlooks Lake Michigan)

_9 **St. Mesrob Armenian Apostolic Church, Racine**
(diamond-shaped nave)

_9 **St. Paul's Episcopal Church, Beloit**
(dramatic altar cross)

_9 **Welsh Hills, Wales**
(Welsh spirituality in the rolling hills of Kettle Moraine)

Episcopal Sites

DeKoven Center

The 34-acre campus of the DeKoven Center was modeled after the typical English college campus when it was built between 1852 and 1876. Today it is the only 19th-century quadrangle (four-sided enclosure surrounded by buildings) in the United States. Opened as an Episcopal school named Racine College, it thrived under the leadership of Father James DeKoven, the only Anglican to be nominated for sainthood. An ardent ritualist, DeKoven was responsible for the Episcopal Church's inclusion of its Catholic heritage in its doctrine and worship.

St. Johns Chapel at the DeKoven Center, Racine

During the early 1900s, the college was a military school (General William "Billy" Mitchell, for whom the county airport is named, scratched his name on a pew in the chapel with a penknife; his work of graffiti has been preserved). Frank Kellogg (as in breakfast cereal) also attended there. The college was forced to close for a time during the Great Depression. Then, the DeKoven Foundation for Church Work was developed in the mid-1930s, and the college became a retreat and conference center.

Today DeKoven offers a wide selection of services, programs, and workshops, both religious and secular. To visit the campus is to take a step back in time. St. John's Chapel (1864) has antiphonal seating (pews that face each other), designed for recitation of the Psalms, and original stained and Belgian glass windows. Outside the chapel is the tomb of Blessed DeKoven, a point of pilgrimage for Episcopalians and other Christians from around the world. Taylor Hall (1867) has enough sleeping rooms for 58 guests. A gymnasium built in 1875 and a swimming pool installed in 1913 are open to the public with no membership required.

Located at 600 21st Street (on Lake Michigan), Racine, Racine County, (262) 633-6401. dekovencenter.pair.com/index.html

Nashotah House Seminary Grounds

Bishop Jackson Kemper and James Lloyd Brech founded Nashotah House Seminary Grounds in 1842. It was the first institution of higher learning in the state.

The Red Chapel (also known as St. Sylvanus Chapel) was built in 1843, making it one of the oldest still-standing churches in the state. Bishop Kemper lived in its basement during the winter of 1844. Today it is used for Sunday services year-round and daily during the summer.

The Chapel of St. Mary the Virgin was opened in 1862 but extensively renovated in 1893. At that time, collegiate-style choir stalls (antiphonal seating) were installed. The chapel, which is listed on the National Register of Historic Places, features two side chapels and is used regularly throughout the year.

Michael, a one-ton bell tuned to the key of F, was dedicated to the college in 1884. It still rings six days a week at 7:30 a.m., noon, and 4:30 p.m. The cloister (Sabine Hall) was originally built with the help of an anonymous benefactor who turned out to be Alice Sabine Magee of Philadelphia. The building burned and was rebuilt in 1910-1911.The seminary is located on 460 acres of Kettle Moraine woodlands and futures a bookstore, a nature trail, and Stations of the Cross.

Located at 2777 Mission Avenue at Mill Road, off County CC on Upper Nashotah Lake, west of Delafield, Waukesha County, (262) 646-6529.

The bell named Michael at the Nashotah House Grounds, near Delafield

Carriage House Chapel

The buildings at this site date back to 1836. They were presented to the Masonic Grand Lodge in 1905 by Willart van Brunt. Episcopal church services were held in the small chapel, called Santa Maria's, over the carriage house. The building is located under the water tower with the Freemasonry symbol. The chapel building is on the National Register of Historic Places. No plans are in place to renovate the chapel, which has been used as farm storage and a barn since being abandoned as a chapel decades ago.

Located on Highway 67 across from Three Pillars, the Masonic rest home in Dousman, Waukesha County (directly beneath the water tower with the Masonic symbol). Contact the Grand Lodge of Wisconsin for more information, (262) 965-2200.

St. Mary's Episcopal Church

St. Mary's had its beginnings with a small group who worshipped together in the loft of a carriage house (see Carriage House Chapel). Later they merged with a group that had been worshipping at the Utica Post Office. Faculty and students walked or rode on horseback eight miles each way from the Nashotah House for services. The current building was erected in 1870. Regular services are held.

Located at 36014 Sunset Drive (Highway 18 at Highway 67), Dousman, Waukesha County, (262) 965-3924.

Early Episcopal Churches

Although the first Episcopal Church in Wisconsin is in Green Bay and the second is in Prairie du Chien, southeast Wisconsin is home to a majority of the oldest and finest Episcopal churches in the state. All but one of the parishes listed here were founded before Wisconsin gained statehood.

St. Matthew's Episcopal Church

This parish was organized in 1839. The building was erected in 1872 and is on the National Register of Historic Places. It features a beautiful wood-carved altar. Regular services are held.

Located at 5900 Seventh Avenue (north of Library Park), Kenosha, Kenosha County, (262) 654-8642. members.tripod.com/suro659/

St. Paul's Episcopal Church, Beloit

With a congregation organized in 1841, this 1848 building is on the National Register of Historic Places. Over the altar is an unusual and beautiful brass crucifix with the image of Christ breaking out of the bounds and coming off the cross. There is a peaceful columbarium downstairs. Regular services are held.

Located at 212 W. Grand Avenue, downtown Beloit, Rock County, (608) 362-4312.

St. John in the Wilderness Episcopal Church

Organized in 1841, the original building was built in a clearing in the woods, hence the name. The cornerstone, laid by Bishop Kemper in 1854, contains a Bible, a prayer book, and copies of that day's newspaper. Regular services are held.

Located at 13 S. Church Street, Elkhorn, Walworth County, (262) 723-4229.

St. John in the Wilderness Episcopal Church, Elkhorn

St. Luke's Episcopal Church, Whitewater

After the first service in 1841, the building was built in 1842 when the parish was officially organized. A bull, the symbol of St. Luke, is featured in the stained glass. Regular services are held.

Located at 146 S. Church (at the corner of Church and Center Streets), Whitewater, Walworth County, (262) 473-8980.

St. Luke's Episcopal Church, Racine

Officially organized in 1842 as a parish, as was its namesake in Whitewater, St. Luke's first services date back to 1835. Its current building was built in 1866 and is on the National Register of Historic Places. The Guild Hall was added in 1906 and the Rectory in 1915. Regular services are held.

Located at 614 S. Main Street, Racine, Racine County, (262) 634-5229.
users.wi.net/stlukes/public_html

St. Alban's Episcopal Church

St. Alban's was erected in 1844 and named for an English martyr-saint; it was organized at the southwest corner of what was called "God's Acre." A marble baptismal font dates to 1870. The English Gothic-style church was patterned after the village church in Peasmarsh, Sussex County, England, the hometown of some of the founders. Regular services are held.

Located at W239 N6440 Maple Avenue (at Main Street),
Sussex, Waukesha County, (262) 246-4430.

St. Matthias Episcopal Church

Organized in 1844 and built in 1851, this church is on the National Register of Historic Places. It is the oldest church in continuing service in Waukesha. Regular services are held.

Located at 111 E. Main Street, downtown Waukesha,
Waukesha County, (262) 547-4838.

Christ Episcopal Church of Delavan

Christ Church, organized in 1844, built its first building in 1850 for $1,200. The existing building was built in 1877 and consecrated in 1879. An extensive remodeling of the interior was completed in 1938, with a new pipe organ and altar installed. Regular services are held.

Located at 503 E. Walworth Avenue, Delavan,
Walworth County, (262) 728-5292.

St. Paul's Episcopal Church, Watertown

This 1859 building, on the National Register of Historic Places, features a new gold Celtic cross on its steeple. Because the church was organized on the same day in 1847 as St. Paul's Church in Milwaukee, the two were presented to the first Annual Council of the Diocese of Wisconsin as "twin parishes." Regular services are held.

Located at 413 S. Second Street, Watertown,
Jefferson County, (920) 261-1150.

St. John Chrysostom Episcopal Church

This uniquely designed, red Gothic Revival structure was built in 1851 and is on the National Register of Historic Places. It is adjacent to St. John's Military

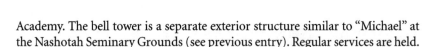

Academy. The bell tower is a separate exterior structure similar to "Michael" at the Nashotah Seminary Grounds (see previous entry). Regular services are held.

Located at 111 Genesee Street, Delafield, Waukesha County, (262) 646-2727.
justus.anglican.org/resources/pc/bios/dekoven/dekoven2.html

Holy Trinity Episcopal Church

This uniquely red and white wooden Gothic Revival church was built in 1871. You can view the interior by stopping at the rectory next door. Regular services are held.

Located at 315 E. Jefferson Street, Waupun,
Dodge County, (920) 324-5700.

Congregational/ United Church of Christ Sites

Spire of the Great Spirit Chapel at the
Cedar Valley Retreat Center, West Bend

Cedar Valley Retreat Center

This United Church of Christ retreat center combines elements of Christian and Native American spirituality into a unique experience. Created by Rev. L. Riesch of West Bend, Cedar Valley Center encompasses 100 acres in the Kettle Moraine area. There is a traditional chapel, a Native American sweat lodge, a log house, a spring-fed pond and creek, and a labyrinth designed by a Capuchin monk. The facilities reopen for seminars, workshops, and retreats.

The Great Spirit Chapel is a four-sided tepee formed out of cement and decorated with stained glass windows and Biblical passages. Susan Kolb, spiritual director, said Reisch wanted to honor the legend that after simultaneously wounding the same deer with a bullet and an arrow, a white man and a Native American chose to share the meal and decided to live side by side in peace. The inside of the chapel fits about a dozen worshippers, and its walls, says Kolb, are covered with "layers of prayers."

Cedar Valley is Christian and ecumenical, "but open and affirming of all faiths," says Kolb. "People can find God in their own way here."

No longer directly affiliated with Cedar Valley, Reisch has built the Futuristic People's Chapel down the street, and next to it, a log replica of the original St. John's UCC. (Reisch serves as pastor of St. John's UCC at County WW and Beaver Dam Road nearby. This church dates back to 1850.) Faith Haven, the property that includes the Futuristic People's Chapel and the log replica, also features an eclectic variety of spiritual art, wrought iron sculptures, and a gift shop.

Cedar Valley located at 5349 County D, northwest of West Bend, Washington County, (888) 450-9202. Faith Haven located at 5519 County D, (262) 629-5435. cedarcampuses.org/cv.htm

Lebanon, Wisconsin's Pomeranian Pilgrim Settlement

William Woltmann, Pomeranian Congregationalist pastor, chose the biblical name Lebanon for this Christian settlement in the New World, noting that the native pines there were reminiscent of the cedars of Lebanon. It was settled in fall 1843.

St. Paul's United Church of Christ

The oldest evangelical and reformed congregation in the state, St. Paul's con-gregation gathered in 1840 and erected the present building in 1880 on the original three-acre site donated by one of its founders. It is now affiliated with the United Church of Christ. Regular services are held.

Located at 495 St. Augustine Road (at Monches Road), Colgate,
Washington County, (262) 628-2319. nconnect.net/stpucc

St. John's United Church of Christ

St. John's United Church of Christ still houses the congregation formed in 1843. The building, originally St. Johannes Evangelical Kirche, was erected in 1868. Regular services are held.

Located at N104 W14181 Donges Bay Road (at Highway 145),
Germantown, Washington County, (262) 251-0640.

First Congregational Church, Janesville

Built in 1848, this building is on the National Register of Historic Places. The congregation first gathered in 1845, making this one of the oldest Congregationalist churches in the state. It is now affiliated with the United Church of Christ. Regular services are held.

Located at 54 S. Jackson Street, downtown Janesville, Rock County, (608) 752-8716.

Shopiere Congregational Church

This building was erected in 1850, making it the second oldest Congregationalist church in the state. It is also on the National Register of Historic Places. Regular services are held.

Located at 5328 E. Church Street (at Buss Road), Shopiere, Rock County, (608) 362-2942.

Fulton Congregational Church

Built along a beautiful high shore of Turtle Creek, this Congregationalist church building was erected in 1857. It is on the National Register of Historic Places. Regular services are held.

Located at 9209 Fulton Drive (one block off Highway 184), village of Fulton,
approximately four miles southwest of Edgerton, Rock County, (608) 884-8512.

First Congregational Church, Waukesha

This imposing red structure at what is now one of the busier intersections of Waukesha was erected in 1867. The building is on the National Register of Historic Places, and the congregation is now part of the United Church of Christ. Planted in front is a "Peace Post." The Peace Post is a simple post with "May Peace Prevail on Earth" on all four sides and in four different languages. These posts are planted with interfaith prayer dedication services throughout the world. At least one other is planted in Wisconsin, at Unity of Madison, in Monona.

Located at 100 E Broadway (at Main Street), Waukesha,
Waukesha County, (262) 542-8008.
execpc.com/wcongucc/fcucc.htm

First Congregational Church, Kenosha

Overlooking Kenosha Library Park, this impressive structure was built in 1874. In the narthex is a small antique organ that traveled 150,000 miles by sea during World War II, its music leading worship for Catholics, Protestants, and Jews. Regular services are held.

Located at 5934 Eighth Avenue, Kenosha,
Kenosha County, (262) 654-0457.

Catholic Sites

Holy Hill National Shrine of Mary

"Come to Holy Hill where your heart can see forever," they say. Indeed, Holy Hill is a sightseeing destination for more than 500,000 people of all faiths each year. At 1,340 feet above sea level and 250 feet above the land around it, it can be seen on a clear day from I-94, north of Delafield.

Founded in 1863 and operated by the Discalced Carmelite Friars, the shrine is located in the beautiful Kettle Moraine area. According to tradition, Pere Marquette planted the first cross in the area on Holy Hill in 1673 on his historic journey to the Mississippi River. He dedicated the spot as "holy ground forever." Later, according to legend, Francois Soubrio arrived from France seeking a sacred hilltop. He became ill and was paralyzed but managed to climb to the summit of this hill, where he was cured. Some say that Soubrio's ghost can still be seen kneeling at the crosses on dusky evenings.

Stories of Holy Hill's healing powers began to spread. Miraculous healings have been reported through the years. Today, a wall in the main chapel displays crutches and braces left behind by people who have found cures at the site.

Today the site houses a huge German Gothic church, a Lourdes grotto, life-sized Stations of the Cross, a cemetery, a café, group retreat facilities, guest rooms, a picnic area, and a monastery. The church is visible for miles around.

The site's best-known physical feature is probably the observation tower, connected to the main chapel, which offers an extraordinary view 178 steps up. (There are spots to peek out if you can't make it all the way to the top.) The tower provides a panoramic view of the county. Holy Hill is open year-round. Autumn is a favorite time to make this trip, but the scenery is such that it's quite beautiful any time of the year. Religious concerts, arts and crafts fairs, and other events are offered throughout the year.

Groups of more than 15 are asked to notify Holy Hill ahead of their visit. Admission and parking are free, but a $2 donation is requested for the observation tower. The cafeteria is open from June through October. For overnight accommodations, make advance arrangements. Regular services are held.

Located at 1525 Carmel Road, Hubertus, 5 miles south of Hartford on Highway 167, Washington County, (262) 628-1838. holyhill.com

Holy Hill National Shrine of Mary, Hubertus

St. Francis Retreat Center

This sanctuary and retreat is host to Calvary Grotto, a Lourdes Grotto, Stations of the Cross, a replica of Portinucula Chapel (the Italian church where St. Francis began the Franciscan Order; the chapel contains relics of St. Francis), and a Shrine to Our Lady of Czestochowa. There are exquisite wood carvings in the main chapel.

St. Francis began as a seminary in 1929. Because the chapel contained pictures of Our Lady of Czestochowa and Our Lady of Ostrobrama, it became a center of pilgrimage for Polish pilgrims. Bordered on two sides by the Fox River, the 160-acre retreat center is serene and visually magnificent. The Lourdes Grotto contains walk-through caves with mosaic images inside. Gardens and religious statues grace the property. St. Francis offers a wide variety of programs, workshops, and retreats for men, women, and businesses. A meeting room accommodates up to 200 people, and there are 56 single rooms for overnight guests.

Located at 503 S. Brown's Lake Drive, 3 miles east of Burlington, Racine County, (262) 763-3600. ofm-abvm.org/SFRC.htm

Siena Center

A Dominican complex on Lake Michigan north of Racine founded in 1960, the Siena Center was named for the 14th-century St. Catherine of Siena, "A Dominican of great religious depth and influence." Siena Center features indoor and outdoor labyrinths, more than 40 acres of grounds, an impressive collection of religious art, and a bookstore with a wide selection of spiritual books, tapes, and gifts. Workshops on motherhood, Taize Prayer, Earth spirituality, spiritual discernment, prayer and Biblical spirituality, and many other interests are offered.

The retreat features 80 private bedrooms and several lounges and meeting rooms. It is open year-round except for three weeks during August.

Located at 5635 Erie Street (at Siena Center Road), north of Wind Point, Racine County, (262) 639-4100. racinedominicans.org

St. Benedict Abbey

Benedictine fathers who owned the south half of the lake established the monastery and seminary in 1945. The lake was also named Shangri-La, after the mythical utopia. Now Shangri-La is the name of the north part of the lake and Benet Lake is the name of the south part (*benet* is Old English for "Benedict").

Our Faith Press Publishing, founded in 1897 by the Order, was founded at this site. Now the monastery supports a mission in Mexico and participates in retreats and pilgrimages.

Inside there is a small "Scripture Museum" with dioramas reflecting various events in the Old Testament and in the life of Christ. Saints' relics as well as relics of the Cross are also on display. *Christ in Man*, a striking mural painted in 1964, depicts Old- and New-Testament figures, saints, and symbols of the major religions of the world. The mural is located in the retreat center dining room.

*Located at 12605 224th Avenue, Benet Lake, Kenosha County
(the Benet Lake office building is nearer the road and
shares the driveway), (262) 396-4311. benetlake.org*

Schoenstatt Center

Waukesha's Schoenstatt Center is one of seven Schoenstatt shrines in the United States (four of which are in Wisconsin) and one of more than 130 worldwide. They are all exact replicas of the Mother Shrine located near the Rhine River near Coblenz, Germany. Dedicated in 1964, Waukesha's Center is the Father House in the United States and includes a retreat center and convent. It is also the national headquarters for the Schoenstatt lay movement.

Founded by Rev. J. Kentenich, who died in 1968, the shrines are dedicated to Mother Thrice Admirable, Queen and Victress of Schoenstatt. Thousands of pilgrims visit the shrines each year. The organization says visitors will "escape from the anxious restlessness of the present age and attach ourselves to a place where we feel loved and accepted." Faithful visitors to the shrines are said to be rewarded with three main graces: "devotion to God, inner transformation in Christ, and apostolic fruitfulness."

Among the special features of each of the intimate chapels are a specially designed crucifix, an ornately carved altar, and Schoenstatt's *Picture of Grace* (a painting of Jesus and Mary). Other U.S. shrines are in Texas, New York, and Minnesota.

*Located at W284 N 698 Cherry Lane (at the very end of Cherry Lane),
Delafield, Waukesha County, (262) 547-7733. schsrsmary.org*

*Other Wisconsin shrine locations include 5558 N. 69th Street (Philip Neri), Milwaukee,
(414) 464-0545; 5310 W. Wisconsin Avenue, Milwaukee (no phone);
and 5901 Cottage Grove Road (Schoenstatt Heights), Madison,
(608) 222-7280 (see separate listing in Chapter 5 for the latter).*

Holy Cross Church and Cemetery

This small, modern building (built in 1962) claims to have a relic of the original Mount Calvary Cross. The church was founded by a Holy Cross priest and organized on September 14, 1845 (on the Feast of the Holy Cross) for Belgium immigrants in the area. There is a cemetery at the site that includes, among other beautiful items, a Calvary shrine altar. Regular services are held.

*Located at 5330 County B (at County A), village of Holy Cross, Ozaukee County,
approximately 5 miles northwest of Port Washington, (262) 285-3658.*

St. Rita's Shrine and Holy Rosary Walkway

A shrine at St. Rita's Convent and Church has carvings over the main entrance that symbolize the Seven Sacraments of the Roman Catholic Church. The primary statue of St. Rita is one of the more beautiful devotional statues in the state.

Between the Convent of the Sisters of St. Rita and St. Monica's Senior Citizen Home is a lovely parklike walkway dedicated to Holy Mother Mary. The walkway was designed by artist Achim Klass as an artistic approach to the prayer of the Holy Rosary. There are also Stations of the Cross.

*Located at 4339 Douglas Avenue, Racine,
Racine County, (262) 639-3223.*

St. Lawrence Church

The St. Lawrence Community was established in 1850, and the building was erected in 1859. The church is next to St. Colletta's and is on the National Register of Historic Places. From this hilltop church, on a clear day, St. John the Baptist Church in Jefferson can be seen more than a mile away. Regular services are held.

*Located at 4875 Highway 18, just outside of Jefferson,
Jefferson County, (920) 674-2822.*

St. John the Baptist Church

Located at the highest point in the city, St. John the Baptist Church can be seen from a distance. The first Catholics in the county, who arrived in 1842, organized the church. The original building dates back to 1858 and was purchased by the congregation. It has undergone a number of renovations, including work in 1885, 1908, and 1949. Regular services are held.

*Located at 324 E. North Street, Jefferson,
Jefferson County, (920) 674-2025.*

St. Wenceslaus Church—The Island Church

Built in 1863, the church served families from Bohemia and Germany. It is significant in Wisconsin's architectural heritage. The small church, 24 by 32 feet, is set upon a log foundation and has been compared to primitive Slavic churches of Eastern Europe. The church officially closed in 1891, but it is still open for special Masses and weddings and by appointment. It is also open every fourth Sunday afternoon from May through September. The Island Church Foundation is next door.

Located at Island Church Road and Blue Joint Road, east of Highway 89 and just southeast of Waterloo, Jefferson County. Contact Kate Radke, 807 Canal Road, Waterloo, (920) 478-2206.

World Shrine of Our Lady of the Green Scapular

The central devotional statue of Our Lady of the Green Scapular is a stunning statue by Thedim who designed many lifelike devotional statues throughout the world. It is set above an altar of mosaic and Italian marble. The World Shrine emphasizes four themes: The Nativity of Christ, The Last Supper, The Crucifixion, and Our Lady. The Shrine Museum contains more than 400 items from more than 40 countries.

Located on Highway H, south of Highway 59, Palmyra, Jefferson County.

St. Mary's Church

Located atop a steep hill aptly named "Church Hill," St. Mary's is an immense structure that overlooks Lake Michigan and the first man-made harbor in North America. It features beautiful bronze relief doors. Erected in 1882, St. Mary's is on the National Register of Historic Places. The church has a parish center museum across the street, which is open from 7:30 a.m. to 4 p.m. Monday, Tuesday, Wednesday, and Friday. Regular services are held.

Located at 430 N. Johnson Street, Port Washington, Ozaukee County, (262) 284-5771.

Lake Church

The picturesque town of Lake Church, located at County D and I-43 about midway between Milwaukee and Sheboygan, was named for the church St. Mary of the Lake that was built in 1881 and overlooks Lake Michigan near Harrington Beach. Gravestones in the cemetery go back to 1848. Regular services are still held.

Nativity of Mary Parish

This 1900s Victorian building, built of striking red brick, is on the National Register of Historic Places. Founded in 1876, St. Mary's is the second oldest church in the area. Built atop a high area in Janesville, the large building can be seen from the Rock River and from quite a distance around town. Regular services are held.

Located at 313 E. Wall Street, downtown Janesville,
Rock County, (608) 752-7861. nativitymary.org

*L*utheran Sites
Holy Trinity Church of Freistadt

The oldest Lutheran church in the state is located outside of Thiensville in the community of Freistadt. About 20 families that were fleeing religious persecution settled in the area in 1839. They first built a log church in 1840; the current building was built shortly thereafter. Originally a Lutheran Buffalo Synod church, the congregation joined the Missouri Synod in 1848. Regular services are held. There have been additions to the church, including a school, but the internal and external integrity is well preserved.

Located at 10729 W. Freistadt Road, at the intersection of County F and
County M (Freistadt and Wausaukee Roads), Ozaukee County
(about 3 miles west of Thiensville), (262) 242-2045.

Holy Trinity Church
of Freistadt, Thiensville

Norway Evangelical Lutheran Church

This was the first Norwegian Lutheran congregation in the state, organized in 1843 in a log building. It lays claim to being the oldest Norwegian Lutheran Church in America. The original log church has been relocated to the campus of Luther Seminary in St. Paul, Minnesota. The log building has become a pilgrimage for members of Norway Lutheran Church who seek to preserve the structure there. The current building was built in 1870 up on top of Indian Hill, a hill overlooking Heg Memorial Park. This was used exclusively until 1954 when a new building was built down the hill. Worship is held every Saturday at 5 p.m. during the summer.

The Heg Memorial Park is named for Colonel Hans Christian Heg, the highest-ranking officer from Wisconsin killed in the Civil War. Dedicated to Norwegian American heritage, it has a museum dedicated to early Norwegian life in western Racine County, a "New Norway." It is open weekends and holidays from Memorial Day through Labor Day.

Located at 6321 Heg Park Road, off Highway 36, Waterford, south of Wind Lake, Racine County, (262) 895-2281.

Jefferson Prairie Church

Developed by the first Norwegian settlement in Wisconsin (and the fourth in all of America), Jefferson Prairie congregation formed in 1838, and the building was erected in 1849, making it one of the oldest Lutheran churches in the state. It straddles the Wisconsin-Illinois border, with the current church building in Illinois and the cemeteries and original marker across the street in Wisconsin. It is affiliated with the Southern Wisconsin Synod of the Evangelical Lutheran Church in America. Regular services are held.

Located at 23184 Bergen Road (approximately 4.5 miles south of Clinton), Rock County, (815) 292-3226.

David Star Church

David Star was founded in 1843 when an entire congregation of Lutherans moved to the United States from Prussia. The church's unique logo features a Star of David embedded in a cross. It is now affiliated with the Wisconsin Evangelical Lutheran Synod. Built on a high hill, it can be seen for miles. Regular services are held.

Located at 2740 David's Star Drive (off Church Road). It can be seen from Western Avenue (County T), between County M and County G, Kirchhayn, Washington County, (262) 375-1843.

Heart Prairie Lutheran Church

Follow a winding road on an isthmus between the lakes in the Whitewater Recreational Center and you come to the Heart Prairie Lutheran Church, a Norwegian house of worship that dates back to 1855. A cemetery with many Norwegian names on headstones surrounds this small church, part of the Evangelical Lutheran Church in America. Regular services are held in the summer months. Oil lamplight services are held there the last Sunday of the month at 8:30 p.m. during the summer, to provide a feeling of back-in-time worship.

Located at W8136 Chapel Drive, approximately 5 miles southeast of Whitewater, Walworth County.

Bethany Lutheran Church

This American Federation of Lutheran Churches building houses the oldest sanctuary (altar area) still serving Norwegians of Rock County. The hand-carved altar and sanctuary, from the old West Luther Valley Lutheran Church, date back to 1871 and are listed on the National Register of Historic Places. Regular services are held.

Located on West Church Road, off County T, just south of Brodhead on the border of Rock and Green Counties, (608) 897-4158.

Lutherdale

This modern campground offers a Bible camp, a modern chapel, an outdoor chapel, a conference center, and an adventure/environmental center on Lutherdale Lake. Lutherdale was, they say, "prayed into being" in 1944, making it one of the oldest church camps in the region. It is affiliated with the Evangelical Lutheran Church in America. Meal services and overnight accommodations are available for church groups, schools, scouts, and adults.

Located at N7891 Highway 12, north of Elkhorn, in the Lauderdale Lakes area, Walworth County, (262) 742-2352.

Concordia University

Originally established in urban Milwaukee, Concordia is now located near Lake Michigan in Mequon. Founded in 1881, Concordia University has more than 4,500 students at its Mequon campus and its eight satellite campuses, making it the largest Lutheran university in the United States. Concordia has the largest tracker pipe organ in the state.

This Missouri Synod college dates back to 1881 with the establishment of a Lutheran preparatory school and junior college in Milwaukee. At one time, more than half the pastors in the Missouri Synod Lutheran Church were graduates of Concordia. It became a four-year college in 1978.

Located at 12800 N. Lake Shore Drive at Highland, Mequon, Ozaukee County, (262) 243-5700.

Wisconsin Lutheran Seminary

The seminary opened in 1863 in Watertown. First known as "Wisconsin University," later as "Northwestern University," the college saw a transfer of theology students to Concordia Seminary in St. Louis in accordance with an arrangement with the Missouri Synod. But the Wisconsin Synod reopened the seminary in Milwaukee a few years later, and remained in various locations in Milwaukee until 1893. A larger seminary building was built in Wauwatosa in 1893.

The present building complex began in 1929. The central building was built to resemble the architecture of the Wartburg, where Martin Luther, founder of the Lutheran religion, translated the New Testament into German. The seminary is affiliated with the Wisconsin Evangelical Lutheran Synod.

Located at 11831 N. Seminary Drive (south of Freistadt Road and west of Green Bay Road), Mequon, Ozaukee County, (262) 242-8100.

Presbyterian Sites

Welsh Hills of Waukesha County

In the 1840s, a Welsh community developed in the rich soil of the rolling hills of western Waukesha County with the village of Wales at its center. The beautiful countryside is at the southern edge of the great Kettle Moraine left by the glacier. The first Presbyterian chapel coincides with the first Welsh settlements in 1842. Bronyberllan, the farm of Richard "King" Jones, where the first services were held, straddles County G (about a mile east of the village of Wales) with a beautiful tree-lined promenade that provided a warm reception to the Welsh settlers.

The first "Gymanfu Ganu" (Welsh singing festival) in Wisconsin was hosted by the Bronyberllan congregation in 1844. Bryn Mawr or Big Hill became the site for the annual homecoming Day of Hillside Preaching and the "Gymanfu Ganu" from 1915 to 1929. The event attracted distinguished preachers and church singers. In the mid-1920s, 2,000 to 3,000 Welsh attended. In 1925, 21 states and two foreign countries were represented. Bryn Mawr Road (which intersects with County G east of Wales) leads up to the 1,050-foot elevation that qualifies as a Welsh mountain. Although it was at one time near Bethania Chapel, it is now a residential subdivision.

Because the Welsh believed churches should be neighborhood places of worship, there were five other congregations by the 1850s in the Welsh hills. By 1873, the number was 10, serving a population of about 1,000: Bethania, Bethesda, Jerusalem, Moriah, Salem, Tabernacle, Union, Zoar, and Zion. The first church, Chapel Log (log church), became Jerusalem Chapel, which eventually was moved to the village of Wales. At the site, which is now Jerusalem Cemetery (on Highway 83 at County G), there is a centennial marker in the front on the gravestones that reads, "Here stood Chapel Log, dedicated July 20, 1845. The church society was organized in 1842. The oldest Welsh Presbyterian Church west of the Great Lakes. 1842-1942."

Three church buildings remain of the Welsh congregations.

Jerusalem Presbyterian (USA) Church (est. 1842)

This stone building, with a beautiful interior, wooden congregational-style pews, simple wooden altar, and large colorful stained glass on either side, is actually the third Jerusalem Chapel; it was built in 1912 and dedicated in 1913. The first framework building and subsequent chapels were built at the Chapel Log site. The old building was finally dismantled in 1925. Sunday worship at 9 a.m.

Located at 207 Main Street, village of Wales,
Waukesha County, (262) 968-3408.

Bethesda United Presbyterian Church (est. 1845)

This is a white Gothic Revival church with an original stone wall that surrounds the parking lot. The Kettle Moraine Parish office is housed here.

Located on County DT at County DE, just south
of the railroad tracks and west of Waukesha,
Waukesha County, (262) 968-3849.

Bethesda United Presbyterian Church, Waukesha

Zion Presbyterian (USA) Church (est. 1873)

This congregation is at the northern edge of the Welsh Hills. Currently, a small modern wood and brick building is at the site.

Located at N13 W28771 County G at I-94, approximately 2.5 miles southwest of Pewaukee, Waukesha County, (262) 646-3256.

Two cemeteries established by the Welsh congregations remain.

Salem Presbyterian Cemetery (formerly Salem Presbyterian Chapel)

Across Highway 83 from Jerusalem Cemetery is the site of Salem Chapel. At the corner of Wales Road (Highway 83) and Welsh Road, the cemetery also posts community announcements.

Located at the corner of Wales Road (Highway 83) and Welsh Road, Wales.

Tabernacle Cemetery (formerly Tabernacle Presbyterian Chapel)

Located well off County G north of Highway 18, northeast of Wales.

First Presbyterian Church, Racine

Erected in 1851, this Greek Revival structure is a national landmark. A plaque on the building states, "Authorities praised the sincerity and refinement of design, high quality of workmanship, overall effect of quiet elegance and repose." Its architect, Lucas Bradley, was a church elder in the congregation. It was recorded by the Historic American Buildings Survey, is listed in the National Register of Historic Places, and is a City of Racine Registered Landmark. Regular services are held.

Located at 716 College Avenue, downtown Racine, Racine County (kitty-corner from Olympia Brown Unitarian Universalist Church (listed later in this chapter), (262) 632-1686.
racinecounty.com/historic/first.htm

Baptist Sites

St. Paul Missionary Baptist Church

One of the oldest African-American churches in the state, St. Paul features a library of its history. It was built in 1857. A new facility across the street features a chapel, classrooms, and activities for neighborhood children, as well as crisis intervention and family programs. Regular services are held.

Located at 123 Center Avenue, downtown Racine,
Racine County, (262) 632-1467.

First Baptist Church of Merton

The oldest Baptist church in the area, built in 1845, this Gothic Revival church is a unique white clapboard meetinghouse with octagonal cupolas and spires. The building is well known in architectural circles and has been mentioned in several publications. Regular services are held. Affiliated with the General Association of Regular Baptist Churches.

Located at 6996 Main Street, at County VV,
Merton, Waukesha County, (262) 538-1464.

First Baptist Church of Merton

Eastern Orthodox Sites

St. Nicholas Orthodox Church

St. Nicholas Russian Orthodox congregation was organized in 1912, and the building was built in 1929 in what is now a residential area of Kenosha. The church is dedicated to Saint Nicholas the Archbishop of Myra, the patron saint of children, sailors, and travelers—who would later become known by the Western Church as Santa Claus. Visitors to the church are asked not to smoke in the vicinity and not to chew gum or talk loudly. Men are asked to remove their hats. Now it is a congregation of the Orthodox Church in America. Regular services are held.

Located at 4313 18th Avenue at 43rd Street, Kenosha, Kenosha County, (262) 657-3415.

St. Mesrob Armenian Apostolic Church

Starting in 1912, Armenian Orthodox in Racine worshipped in St. Luke's Episcopal Church. The congregation purchased an existing church building on State Street in 1924. The present complex, which seats 250 in a diamond-shaped nave and altar area and large hall, was built in 1973. The church was named for St. Mesrob, the founder of the Armenian alphabet.

Located at 4605 Erie Street, Racine, Racine County, (262) 639-0531. execpc.com/stmesrob/ Another Armenian Orthodox congregation, St. Hagop, is located nearby at 4100 Newman Road, Racine, (262) 632-2033.

Zion Orthodox Hermitage—Russian Orthodox Church Outside of Russia

Father Anthony, a monk, founded this little hermitage in 1994. It's located in the oldest house of worship in the community, the 130-year-old former St. Mark's schoolhouse. The building was moved to the site in 1994. It contains a simple but elegant little chapel. The hermitage can also house a few people for retreats. Call ahead for service times and further information.

Located on County Q less than a mile west of County K, Richwood, Dodge County, (920) 262-8800.

Interior of the chapel at Zion Orthodox Hermitage, Richwood

St. Mary and St. Antonios Coptic Church

This, the only Coptic Orthodox church in Wisconsin, features icons and ethnic music in the regular services held in the Coptic language with some English.

Located at 124 N. Third, Waterford, Racine County, (262) 534-2873. angelfire.com/al/stantoniouscoptic/

Other Christian Sites

Kingdom of Voree and the "Strangite Mormons"

James Jesse Strang founded this sizeable settlement of the Church of Jesus Christ of Latter Day Saints around 1844, and the area was inhabited until 1865.

Strang, both famous and infamous in his day, was appointed to succeed Mormon Church founder Joseph Smith Jr. as the leader of the church and was told by Smith that he was to "plant a stake of Zion in Wisconsin in the lands of Racine and Walworth."

The story of what happened after that varies greatly depending on who is doing the reporting. On September 13, 1845, after a vision, Strang and a group of his followers uncovered three brass plates buried near an oak tree near the White River in Walworth County, an area called Voree. Considered a prophet and a seer, Strang quickly translated the unknown language on the plates. Among the phrases on the plate were "Record my words, and bury it in the Hill of Promise."

The hill became known as the Hill of Promise, and the Kingdom of Voree grew at its foot to become a thriving community of more than 2,000 people, all of them Latter Day Saints. Its inhabitants farmed and provided printing services, shoemaking, plough manufacturing, and dog breeding. It is claimed that an inhabitant of Voree made the discovery that tomatoes are edible rather than poisonous.

Later, Strang moved his followers, later known as the "Strangite Mormons," to Beaver Island, near Michigan's Upper Peninsula, where he pronounced himself king. He was shot there in 1856. Some of his followers evolved into what is now the Reorganized Church of Jesus Christ of Latter Day Saints, which considers itself separate from the Church of Jesus Christ of Latter-day Saints headquartered in Utah.

Some descendents still live in the area, and one of the original stone houses in Spring Prairie is still occupied.

Located 2 miles west of Burlington on Highway 11 at the White River, designated by a stone marker, along the Walworth and Racine County line. strangite.org/Wisconsin.htm

Union Church

Several religious denominations joined together to build a church in an area of northern Racine County they called Union Church. Today, Union Church is just a name on the map without a single church.

Covenant Harbor (Geneva Bay Centre)

Covenant Harbor is an Evangelical Christian camp and retreat just outside town in Lake Geneva. The Central Conference of the Evangelical Mission Covenant Church of America purchased the land in 1947. The site features its original guesthouse, carriage house, gatehouse, hilltop house, and boathouse from what was the George Sturges property, purchased in 1881.

Today, Covenant Harbor offers summer youth camps, adult and family camps and retreats, day camps, an Elderhostel, adventure programs, and more. Covenant Harbor's vision is to be "a sanctuary where diverse people meet God in a well-developed and enriching environment stewarded by a competent, responsive, well-cared-for team of God-honoring people."

Located at 1724 Main Street, Lake Geneva,
Walworth County, (262) 248-3600.

Moravian Church of Watertown

This beautiful and traditional Moravian church is nestled in a neighborhood of lovely churches in Watertown. The Gothic castle-like church building dates back to 1854 and is one of the oldest in the state. The other churches include the domed **St. James Wisconsin Synod Lutheran Church** and **St. John's Evangelical Lutheran Church** with its traditional steeple. Also within these few blocks on the west side of Watertown is **St. Henry Catholic Parish**, which dates back to 1843.

Located at 510 Cole, Watertown, Jefferson County, (920) 261-7494.

Moravian Church of Watertown

Native American Sites

Aztalan Village State Park

A Native American culture occupied this 21-acre village of 500 people from 1000 to 1200 C.E. Timothy Johnson discovered the site in 1836; it would be one of the most significant archaeological finds in the state. It features three pyramid-shaped platform mounds, conical mounds, and a large, protective stockade, all along the banks of the Crawfish River.

Parts of the site have been reconstructed. Because many ancient Mississippian and/or Woodland villagers are buried there, modern Native Americans consider the site sacred. The area still draws many for solstice and equinox meditations and small ceremonies.

Plenty of theories exist about the complex, organized civilization that lived in this city for hundreds of years and then disappeared. According to some, its inhabitants practiced human sacrifice and ritual cannibalism. Later, they burned the city to the ground. A museum dedicated to the site is located nearby, at the intersection of Counties Q and B. It is open 10 a.m. to 5 p.m. from May through mid-October.

Located in Aztalan State Park, on County B, just south of I-94, 3 miles east of Lake Mills, Jefferson County. Museum is located at N6264 County Q, east of Lake Mills. Call Friends of Aztalan, (920) 648-8774. madison.k12.wi.us/whitehorse/ss/intro.htm

The Great Solar Mound at Aztalan State Park, Lake Mills

Miracle, the White Buffalo

Born on August 20, 1994, a little snow-white buffalo calf shocked the Heider family of Janesville. The family had been raising buffalo for five years and knew that the birth of a white buffalo is exceedingly rare. But within days of the event, the baby buffalo became known around the country as the fulfillment of a Native American prophecy that says the birth of a white buffalo will usher in an age of harmony and balance.

Miracle, as the buffalo was named, proceeded to change colors, also according to prophecy—black in January of 1995, red in June of 1995, and yellow in November of 1995 (it is said that each color represents a race of humankind). According to the legend, the buffalo will turn white again when there is world peace. Hundreds of thousands of people have meditated and prayed at the site, which has become a shrine. Miracle's corral is decorated with thousands of Native American dream catchers, tobacco pouches, prayer cloths, medals, pictures, and a variety of religious icons. In 1998, Miracle gave birth to a reddish calf, which was named Millennium.

Visitors are welcome, free of charge, from 10 a.m. to 5 p.m. seven days a week, but are asked to call first. A freewill offering is taken. There is a small museum and gift shop at the site. No cameras of any kind are allowed. Overnight camping is allowed in the pasture next to Miracle—call Buffalo Dude at the following number to make reservations.

Located on the Heider Farm, 2739 S. River Road, just southwest of Janesville, Rock County. From I-90, get off at Avalon Road (exit 277), and go 4 miles west to River Road; turn right, (608) 752-2224. homestead.com/WhiteBuffaloMiracle

Peninsula Park

A large Menominee Indian village existed at this site for thousands of years, until 1831. The original site extended north to the area of what is now Triangle Park. Father Joseph Marest, a missionary priest and the first nonnative to live among the villagers in 1698, is said to have erected a large wooden cross in what is the middle of the park. The area is flat, open, and serene.

Located at Ulau and Clay Streets (on the Milwaukee River), Saukville, Ozaukee County.

Two Potawatomi Lakes

Tichigan Lake, in Racine County, derives its name from the Potawatomi word for "Home of the Dead." There is said to be a native graveyard located in the area.

Phantom Lake, adjacent to Mukwonago in Waukesha County, has a Potawatomi name, *Nish-ke-tash*, which means "Lake of Mystery." There are native legends of love and death connected with the lake.

Mound Sites

Lizard Mound County Park

This park contains 31 effigy mounds (surviving out of an original 60) and is named for the most outstanding mound—a lizard mound, hundreds of feet long. The park has one of the largest, most diverse groups of effigy mounds open to the public in Wisconsin. This grouping includes the huge lizard mound and 11 panther effigies.

Located on low ground, not near a body of water, this group of mounds has an unusual location; the vast majority of mounds were built adjacent to lakes and rivers because of the spiritual significance of such areas. But springs surround the area, and Native Americans considered springs to be entrances to the underworld. Some of the mounds here date back to 500 C.E., but they are among the best-preserved mounds in the state.

Visitors can take a self-guided, mile-long tour of the park of 25 mounds. Mounds are well preserved and plainly marked, and information is provided on markers.

Located on County A, east of Highway 144, northwest of West Bend, Washington County, Washington County Parks phone, (262) 335-4445.

A panther effigy at Lizard Mound County Park, West Bend

Pike Lake Effigy Mounds

Several mounds can be found around Pike Lake, in the Kettle Moraine State Forest. The east side of the lake was a campsite used by Chief Kewaskum, the famous Potawatomi. The area is part of the Ice Age National Scenic Trail and also features Powder Hill, a 1,350-foot glacial ridge, which provides a panoramic view of the area's unique topographic features.

Located at 3544 Kettle Moraine Road, Pike Lake State Park (due north of Holy Hill and south of Highway 60), near Hartford, Washington County.

Jefferson County Indian Mounds and Trail Park

Also known as the General Atkinson Mound Group, Jefferson County Indian Mounds features 11 of 72 original mounds, including four turtles, two birds, a tadpole, and a pear-shaped and three conical mounds. They range in size from 75 to 222 feet long. The mounds in this park date back 1,500 years and are well preserved and well marked with informational plaques. Fort Atkinson businessman Hugh Highsmith, who purchased the land containing the mounds, then donated the land to Jefferson County for the park in 1997. Other mounds also surround Lake Koshkonong but are on nonpublic land.

Located on Lake Koshkonong west of Highway 26, approximately 6 miles southwest of Fort Atkinson, Jefferson County (take Old State 26 to Koshkonong Mound Road; the park will be on the left just past Vinnie Ha Ha Road). A historic marker is visible at the parking area. More information is available at the Hoard Historical Museum, 407 Merchants Avenue, Fort Atkinson, (920) 563-1870.

Panther Intaglio

This is the only known intaglio effigy—the reverse of a mound, excavated for ceremonial reasons, circa 1000 C.E. Part of the tail has been covered. Of the other 10 recorded intaglios, all have been destroyed. One possible explanation for the existence of an intaglio is that some Native Americans believed water spirits originated below the Earth's surface. Other hypotheses include that the intaglio was filled with water for religious ceremonies or served as a lookout where people would hide to protect a nearby cornfield from animals.

Because the intaglio is located just a few feet from the road that runs along the Rock River, in a residential area, visitors may need to pull off the road and park across the street to view it. There is a marker at the site.

Located on Highway 106 (Riverside Drive) at the western edge of Fort Atkinson, Jefferson County.

Whitewater Effigy Mounds Park

Also known as Maples Mound Group, this grouping is on the National Register of Historic Places and includes a panther, mink, turtle, bird, conical, linear, and several oval mound shapes. Although the area is not clearly marked, the mounds are quite accessible, located in a newly developed residential area. The entrance to the park is set back from the road in a clear area.

Located on Effigy Mound Road at Mounds Park, Whitewater, Walworth County.

Beloit College Effigy Mound Group

The oldest continuously running college in the state of Wisconsin was built in the mid-1840s among at least 23 conical, linear, and animal effigy mounds. A turtle mound inspired the symbol for Beloit College.

More than a dozen of the mounds are conical. These mounds are believed to have been built between 700 and 1200 C.E. by ancestors of the Ho-Chunk Nation. All of these mounds have been excavated, and the materials found in them (including pieces of pottery and tools) are available for viewing at the college's Logan Museum of Anthropology.

Located on the grounds of Beloit College, 700 College Street, Beloit, near I-90 and I-43 near the Illinois border. Watch for signs in the city to direct you to the college. beloit.edu/museum/publicart/publicmounds.htm; admiss.beloit.edu/turtletalk/mounds.html

Cutler Mound Group

This mound group now consists of three conical burial mounds that date back 2,000 years; they are directly in front of the Waukesha Public Library in the middle of the city. The center mound is nine feet high and 65 feet in diameter. Excavations in the mid-1800s showed that one of the mounds had been built over a large in-ground burial chamber and uncovered fragments of a human skeleton, decorative pipes, and pieces of shell and pottery. There were once 411 mounds in the Waukesha County.

Located on Maple Avenue and Cutler Street in Cutler Park, Waukesha, Waukesha County.

Mounds at Cutler Park, Waukesha

Turtle Mound (Indian Mound Reservation Boy Scout Camp)

One of a twin formation at Silver Lake, this well-preserved turtle effigy is located on the south shore in the Indian Mound Reservation Boy Scout Camp. Although surveyed in the 1850s, the north shore twin's status is now unknown, and it is presumed destroyed.

The Milwaukee County Council Boy Scout Camp also features an interfaith chapel across the path from Turtle Mound. There is an emphasis on respect for the mound. The camp is used year-round by the Boy Scouts and other related groups.

*Located on Silver Lake, the village of Summit Corners,
Waukesha County (near Delafield), north of I-94,
(262) 567-6229.*

Unitarian Universalist Sites

Olympia Brown Unitarian Universalist Church

This church was founded in 1842 as The Universalist Society of Racine. The building, erected in 1851, was the first building on Monument Square and the third church built in what was then known as Port Gilbert. It was named for the first woman in the United States ordained in a recognized church. Rev. Olympia Brown served as minister here from 1878 to 1887. Regular services are held.

*Located at 625 College Avenue, downtown Racine near
the Root River, Racine County, (262) 634-0659.*

Bradford Community Church Unitarian Universalist

This church was named for Mary Bradford, an early local educator and advocate of women's rights. The congregation meets in its original beautiful stone historic building that was recently reacquired. Regular services are held.

*Located at 5810 Eighth Avenue, downtown Kenosha, Kenosha County
(north of Library Park and near the post office), (262) 656-0544.
bradforduuchurch.homestead.com/Home.html*

United Unitarian and Universalist Church

On the National Register of Historic Places, the building was erected in 1878. Regular services are held.

*Located at 216 Main Street, Mukwonago,
Waukesha County, (262) 363-5686.*

Jewish Sites

Aguda Achim Chabad Cemetery and Synagogue

This historic Orthodox Jewish cemetery is located in Cudahy, but the congregation that developed it is now located in Mequon.

The congregation started in 1902 with 18 Polish Jews who had just arrived in America. First services were held at 52 Cherry Street downtown. Later they moved to North 11th Street. A new synagogue was built in 1954 at 5820 W. Burleigh Street, and services were held there for the next 40 years. The new, contemporary-style building was erected in 1996. Services are held Sunday mornings, weekdays, and Fridays at sunset.

Cemetery located at 3690 E. College Avenue, Cudahy, Milwaukee County, (414) 242-2236. Synagogue located at 2233 W. Mequon Road, Mequon, Ozaukee County, (262) 242-2235.

Olin-Sang-Ruby Union Institute (OSRUI)

Founded in 1951 by the Union of American Hebrew Congregations, this camp serves much of North America. The camp sits on more than 200 acres alongside Lac Labelle. About 1,000 campers of all ages attend the camp each year. In addition to typical camp activities (horseback riding, sports, and boating), there are Judaic activities with rabbis and/or educators. The camp mission is "Jewish Learning through Jewish Living." The grounds feature many fine pieces of contemporary Jewish art emphasizing religious and cultural themes.

Located at 600 Lac La Belle Drive, Oconomowoc, Waukesha County, (262) 567-6277. uahc.org/camps/olinsangruby/html/index.htm

Islamic Sites

Masjid Tawheed-American Albanian Islamic Center

Masjid Tawheed (literally, "One God") was established in 1996 by the Albanian American Islamic Society. The mosque is located in a rural area. Regular prayers are held.

Located at 6001 88th Avenue (County H) at 60th Street (County K), west of Kenosha, Kenosha County, (262) 654-0575.

The spire of Masjid Tawheed, Kenosha

*E*astern *Religious* *Sites*

Hindu Temple of Wisconsin

Lord Vishnu is the main deity at this brand-new temple opened in the summer of 2000; other deities include Lord Janet, Lord Krishna, Lord Shiva, and Goddess Durga. The only Hindu temple in Wisconsin, it attracts worshippers from throughout southern Wisconsin. It provides a place for individual and congregational worship and serves educational, cultural, and spiritual needs of the Indian community. Regular services are held. Open most evenings.

Hindu Temple of Wisconsin, Pewaukee

What is termed Hinduism is actually a rich variety of Indian beliefs that unfolded over time. Hindus believe that God manifests in many different forms. A common way of understanding God is through a threefold manifestation—Brahma (creator), Vishnu (preserver), and Siva (destroyer)—all manifestations of one God, Janardana. Reincarnation and yoga are two of the concepts Hinduism has made familiar to the West.

Located at N4063 W243 Pewaukee Road (Highway 164), north of Capital Drive, between the towns of Pewaukee and Sussex (next to the large Shepherd of the Hills Lutheran Church), (262) 695-1200. hindutemplewis.com

Jain Religious Center of Wisconsin

Located on the same grounds as the Hindu Temple of Wisconsin, listed previously, this is the only Jain temple in Wisconsin. Built in 2000 to Jain religious specifications where cleanliness is cherished, the main altar and idol were installed in 2001. Jains follow ancient Indian teachings on how to liberate the soul by freeing it of karma. Jains may kill no living things, including animals.

Located at N4063 W243 Pewaukee Road (Highway 164), north of Capital Drive, between the towns of Pewaukee and Sussex (behind the Hindu Temple of Wisconsin), (262) 242-0245. jainwi.org

Original Root Zen Center

The first Zen Buddhist monastery and retreat center in Wisconsin, Original Root Zen Center was founded in 1987, affiliated with the Kwan Um School of Zen (Korean form). Most retreats are silent. The Center is located at Lake Michigan in the DeKoven Center (see Episcopal sites, previous).

Located at 600 21st Street, on the second floor of the East Building (which faces the lake), Racine, Racine County, (262) 638-8580.

Other Sites

Waukesha Healing Springs

In this area there are more than 50 springs said to have special healing powers. In the 1850s spa trade, Colonel Richard Dunbar drank of the springwater and was cured of his ailments. Later, bathhouses and health facilities advertised the "wondrous Waukesha water." Today two of the springs are located in city parks. Of the many springwater bottlers from that time, only Bethesda Roxo

Waters (since 1868) still bottles and sells the healing springwater.

Located at Bethesda Roxo, 574 Elizabeth Street, near Bethesda City Park, Waukesha, Waukesha County. Call the Waukesha Area Convention & Visitors Bureau, (262) 542-0330; (800) 366-8474. ci.waukesha.wi.us/history/page260.htm, ci.waukesha.wi.us/history/topic432.htm

The Recording Angel

This larger-than-life bronze and marble sculpture was created in 1921 by Leonard Taft, designed as a memorial to Clarence Shaler's wife of 26 years. Erected in 1923, it was the first of seven bronze statues installed in the town of Waupun by Shaler. Waupun has been nicknamed "The City of Sculptures," and this serene creation may be the most outstanding of them all. *The Recording Angel*, with her Book of Life, casts a peaceful and contented air around the area. The cemetery seems to fade in the presence of this fabulous piece of art.

Located in Forest Mound Cemetery on N. Madison Street, Waupun, on the border of Fond du Lac and Dodge Counties. For more information, call the Chamber of Commerce, (920) 324-3491.

The Recording Angel, Waupun

Angel Museum

The world's largest collection of angels resides in the former St. Paul's Catholic Church building in Beloit. The angels—more than 12,000 of them—were once the private collection for the Berg family of Beloit and were housed in their ranch-style home. The angels come in an unimaginable array of sizes, designs, and materials—glass, wood, pewter, clay, porcelain. Some are antiques; others are brand new. One is made of Legos.

The museum also features a separate collection of 600 black angels belonging to Oprah Winfrey, as well as a gift shop and a café. The museum advertises its philosophy that angels are "symbols of what is joyful, noble, and good. It refrains from promoting religion or a theology of angels."

Admission for the museum is $5 for adults and $4 for children, with a senior discount available. Open 10 a.m. to 5 p.m. Monday through Saturday, May through September; 10 a.m. to 4 p.m. Tuesday through Saturday, October through April.

Located at 656 Pleasant Avenue, downtown Beloit (across from Beloit College), Rock County, (608) 362-9099. visitbeloit.com/Angelpage.htm

Tyranena (Rock Lake)

Tyranena is an enigmatic underwater holy site that may be related to Aztalan (see Native American Sites section earlier in this chapter). It's said that pyramids were built there in prehistoric times but have since been covered by water. The existence of the mysterious pyramids have neither been definitively proved nor disproved. Some believe that inconclusive aerial photos show unusual formations in Rock Lake, some of them square. Efforts to clarify data have been thwarted by mysterious repeated equipment failures and further inconclusive evidence.

There are records of a headless human effigy mound now covered by the lake's water.

Photographs and eyewitnesses have concurred on one unexplained phenomenon. Large boulders seem to float on the surface in the middle of the lake. This is not a frequent phenomenon, but it occurs often enough to have been studied. There are other unusual phenomena and occurrences that have been documented over the years.

Additionally, tales abound of a lake serpent monster that protects the mysteries of Rock Lake.

Located in Lake Mills, Jefferson County, which has two parks on the lake. From Lake Mills, take County B 1.5 miles, then turn on Rock Lake Road for Upper Rock Lake Park. For Lower Rock Lake Park, turn on Park Lane Road. rocklakeresearch.com/; science-frontiers.com/sf030/sf030p01.htm ; enjoycentralwi.com/lakemills.htm

Namaste Center of Wisconsin

Named after a Hindu phrase meaning, "the god in me recognizes the god in you," the Namaste Center of Wisconsin is an eclectic and humble little retreat. The Center director, Kari Chapman, says the Center was "cocreated with the spirit of God." It features several interfaith meditation trails and ceremonial areas. Crystal healing and mediumship are offered. A newsletter is available. The town of Lake Mills is considered to be located at Stargate 14 (stargates are multidimensional portals that provide an opportunity to move between dimensions), according to Chapman.

Located at W7872 County B, Lake Mills, just across the highway from Rock Lake, Jefferson County, (920) 648-3580. namaste-wi.com

Northeast

Northeast Wisconsin

*Including the counties of Brown, Calumet, Door, Florence,
Fond du Lac, Forest, Green Lake, Kewaunee, Langlade, Manitowoc,
Marinette, Marquette, Menominee, Oconto, Outagamie, Shawano,
Sheboygan, Waupaca, Waushara, and Winnebago*

Chapter 3

Northeast Wisconsin

*T*he Lord shall preserve thy going out and thy coming in,
from this time forth for evermore.

—Psalm 121:8

FATHER JEAN NICOLET thought he had arrived in China when he set foot in the Green Bay region in 1634, the first European to visit. There he met many tribal nations in the region, peacefully coexisting. Although some different tribes would migrate to the region, several tribal nations remain. Menominee, Potawatomi, Stockbridge-Munsee Mohican, Ojibwe, and Oneida have tribal-nation land reserves in this region of Wisconsin.

Over the past few centuries, there have been several missions of various denominations in this region. Some mission churches are honored to this day. Others have been allowed to crumble into decay without tears of regret.

Rock Island, off the tip of Door County, has a very old cemetery; in fact, in this region are several of the oldest cemeteries in Wisconsin, including the oldest Catholic cemetery in Allouez and the Copper Culture Cemetery in Oconto. There are stones with stories here. The medicine wheel of Campbellsport and Menominee's spirit stone are living legacies of the spiritual connectedness to the land.

This region is home to first Christian Science building in the world, the first Episcopal church in the state, and the first Moravian church west of the Great Lakes.

The region's awesome natural beauty leads to many natural sources of sacred space. Naturally, this region is home to more retreat centers and church camps than any other.

Statue of St. Francis of Assisi at St. Lawrence Seminary, Mount Calvary

Favorite Sites

- ☞ **Algoma Boulevard Methodist Church and Nativity Museum, Oshkosh**
  (collection of nativities from all over the world)

- ☞ **Cathedral Church of St. Paul, Fond du Lac**
  (magnificent wood carvings)

- ☞ **Cathedral of Pines, Nicolet National Forest**
  (oldest virgin pine stand in Wisconsin)

- ☞ **Cave Point County Park, Door County**
  (some of the state's most beautiful and inspiring shoreline)

- ☞ **Church of the Assumption of the Blessed Virgin Mary, Pulaski**
  (a big-city church in a small town)

- ☞ **Copper Culture Mound State Park, Oconto**
  (oldest known cemetery in the U.S.)

◡ **Ephraim Church of the Brotherhood, Ephraim**
    (landmark namesake in Door county)

◡ **Loretto Shrine, St. Nazianz**
    (remote and humble little chapel atop a hill)

◡ **Lutheran Indian Mission, Shawano County**
    (mission church still standing with community support)

◡ **Medicine Wheel (Krug-Senn Site), Campbellsport**
    (it's a mystery)

◡ **Monte Alverno Retreat Center, Appleton**
    (Wisconsin's oldest retreat center)

◡ **Old St. Joseph's Church, DePere**
    (award-winning architecture)

◡ **Our Lady of Walsingham Shrine (Grace Church), Sheboygan**
    (an unusual Episcopal shrine with British ties)

◡ **Spirit Rock, Keshena**
    (source of Menominee strength)

◡ **Stavkirke, Washington Island**
    (built to resemble a Viking ship)

◡ **St. Agnes Church, Algoma**
    (wondrous view of Lake Michigan from the
    sanctuary's front doors)

◡ **St. Hubert Shrine, Goodman**
    (nestled deep in the woods)

◡ **St. Lawrence Seminary, Mount Calvary**
    (beautiful relief mural of St. Francis's life)

◡ **St. Mary's Springs Church, Fond du Lac**
    (spring-fed grotto of St. Joseph)

◡ **Thunder Mountain, Marinette County**
    (place where thunderbirds were said to have been born)

◡ **Whistler Mound Group, Hancock**
    (unique enclosure mound group)

Native American Sites

Calumet County Park

Calumet County is named for a Menominee Indian Village that existed on the east shore of Lake Winnebago. *Calumet* is the Menominee word for "peace." The county insignia features two crossed peace pipes and a chain of beads; a sign at the entrance to Calumet County Park shows the insignia and reads, "We extend the calumet to the world." At various times in history, the land has been home to Menominee, Ojibwe, Sauk, Fox, Potawatomi, and Ho-Chunk peoples.

The Ridge Mound Group is located in Calumet County Park. There are six panther mounds from less than 100 feet up to 320 feet. In addition to the mounds, this park features a camper's chapel in the woods, with services Saturdays at 7 p.m. from Memorial Day to Labor Day. The site is on the National Register of Historic Places.

Located at Calumet County Park, N6150 County EE (about 4 miles northwest of Stockbridge), Calumet County, (920) 439-1008.

High Cliff Mounds

Nine mounds remain from a grouping of about 30. They are on the Indian Mound trail in the upper section of the park. Information is posted about lifestyles, vegetation, and animal life in the area along the self-guided trail. A panther mound measures 285 feet. The site features three other panther mounds, two conical mounds, a linear mound, and two buffalo mounds. The trail has a limestone surface and is suitable for disabled visitors. High Cliff State Park is on the National Register of Historic Places. The park is open from 6 a.m. to 11 p.m., but campsites are available.

Located at High Cliff State Park, on the eastern shore of Lake Winnebago, Calumet County. Enter off Highway 114 north of Shorewood, (920) 989-1106.

Butte des Morts

According to the legend of the "Hill of the Dead," Native Americans have always held the Butte des Morts area as sacred. Elaborate ceremonies were held there, and the dead of many different tribes were buried on or near the hill—sometimes long after they had died. Burial and reburial bundles and skeletons have been found showing the dead were brought from a distance to be buried there.

Several major battles were fought in this territory because the land was so fruitful.

Located on Highway 41 at Lake Butte des Morts, Winnebago County.

Smith Park Mound Group

The place where Father Jean Nicolet is said to have first entered Wisconsin and camped in the early 1600s is marked by a monument and plaque on Doty Island. The island was considered sacred long before that. Nearby, at Smith Park, three panther mounds are still visible, measuring 217, 200, and 125 feet. They vary from 1.5 to 2 feet high.

Located at Smith Park, Menasha, Winnebago County.

Whistler Mound Group and Ceremonial Embankment

On the National Register of Historic Places, this site features a unique mound enclosure with a low double-wall embankment measuring 120 feet by 51 feet. It is believed to have been sacred space for ceremonies. There are benches arranged at intervals to sit and meditate (or contemplate) around these unique mounds. "Such enclosures undoubtedly defined sacred spaces where periodic ceremonies were held," says State Archeologist Bob Birmingham.

Located at Whistler Mounds Park, on County FF, east of the village of Hancock at Fish Lake, Waushara County.

Medicine Wheel (Krug-Senn Site)

Discovered in 1986, this site has been the subject of archaeological dispute and research ever since. Some contend that it is a fraud. Others consider the site full of insight and intrigue.

This complex of stone circles and other petroforms has been called Wisconsin's Stonehenge. The 300 stone circles, as well as stone arrangements of animals, calendars, and star constellations, is said to date back 3,500 years —predating the effigy mounds. It is the most complex such arrangement in North America.

The amazing extent of ancient knowledge is evident in the layout of the rocks, which are arranged along equinox and solstice lines, tracking yearly movements of the sun and moon. (They are two degrees off, which can be explained by the passage of time and changes in the Earth's orbit since they were created.)

"The Indian tribes have legends of a place that means the same to Indians as Jerusalem does to Christians," says landowner Robert Krug. He believes that this is that place, and there is evidence to suggest that he is right. For example, many significant effigy mounds, though miles away, are geographically placed to align with this site.

Bob Krug at the Medicine Wheel site, Campbellsport

Visitors to the site will see the rock configurations as well as teaching and cooking areas that were probably designed to serve 1,000 people at a time. Native Americans probably did not live right at the site, but rather traveled there for important festivals, ceremonies, and spiritual events.

Krug, a retired dairy farmer, has become the resident expert of the site, acquiring an extensive knowledge of the stone arrangements and their meaning with the assistance of a variety of archaeologists and Native American spiritual leaders.

The central circle in the arrangement is more than 28 feet in diameter, made up of 62 carefully sized and spaced stones, with two six-stone concentric circles inside. It appears to be the "hub" for seven outlying stone circles. According to astronomical calculations, a prominent bolder inside the circle would have been the precise place where summer and winter solstice lines would have crossed 2,500 years ago. Other stones are placed to serve as solar calendars, casting shadows over the next stone in line every 26 days at high noon.

"Religious rituals, among the most enduring of all cultural traditions, have probably been celebrated on this drumlin by countless clans and generations since ancient times," says Krug in an unpublished article entitled "A Retired Dairy Farmer and an Ancient Drumlin in Fond du Lac County: Bob Krug Uncovers an Early Algonquin Sacred Site," by Jim Graham, Roy Kotynek, Ira Lax, and Bernie Travikar. Krug continues: "Knowledgeable Algonquin-speaking visitors today—from Menominee and Potawatomi to Chippewa (Ojibwe), Fox, Cheyenne, or Cree—all offer different observations, interpretations, and stories about the spiritual significance of particular petroforms here; yet all regard our drumlin as a very sacred site."

Located at 3504 Spring Drive (second farm off County W), approximately 4 miles south of Highway 67 and County W in Campbellsport, Fond du Lac County, (920) 533-8164 or (920) 533-8610. By appointment only. Allow at least four hours to tour.

Thunder Mountain

This high hill in western Marinette County is actually a relic of a mountain range that existed before the Rockies did. It is said to be the birthplace of thunderbirds, giant mythical birds that were created to protect humans from the great serpents. Thunderbirds were said to lay their eggs there, and a number of myths and legends are attached to the site.

According to Potawatomi legend, an Indian hunter happened upon a serpent and a thunderbird fighting there. Both promised greatness to the man who would shoot the other; confused, he shut his eyes and shot the thunderbird. The bird was weakened and taken under the hill as a prisoner. According to Menominee legend, which includes the same story about the hunter shooting the thunderbird, lightning is the flashing of the angry thunderbird's eyes. The stones at the foot of the mountain, they say, are petrified thunderbird eggs.

The native name *Chequah-Bikwaki* ("Thunder Mountain") also refers to the legend that lightning is seen flashing from the top of the mountain whenever there is going to be a thunderstorm. It is also said that footsteps at the top of the mountain can be heard near the bottom. There does seem to be an abundance of peace and quiet, even though all-terrain vehicle tracks are visible on the larger trails.

Thunder Mountain Park, in the town of Stephenson, is an undeveloped area that provides scenic views. The site features a breathtaking lookout over Marinette County.

Located at the end of Thunder Mountain Road in western Marinette County. From Crivitz, go west on County W 14.5 miles to Cauldron Falls Road, then north 3 miles to Thunder Mountain Road. The mountain park is about 1 mile down the road. Marinette County Parks phone: (715) 732-7530.

Sheboygan Indian Mound Park

This 15-acre park, on the National Register of Historic Places, features 18 rare effigy mounds including five deer, two panthers, and three conical mounds. The mounds, circa 500-750 C.E., are well preserved and well marked. A unique feature is an artificial skeleton under glass, to show how the burial mounds would have appeared inside. It is believed there were originally 33 mounds at the site. The site is also known as the Kletzien Mound Group.

The park is dedicated to "those oldest peoples of Wisconsin whose love for their homeland kept it green and beautiful and rich in nature's bounty. May we learn to preserve it twice as well." The park is open from April 1 to November 1.

Located on County KK (South 12th Street), Ninth Street, and Panther Avenue, south of Sheboygan, Sheboygan County, (920) 459-3444.

Copper Culture Mound State Park

This site was discovered by an Oconto resident in 1952. Native Americans gathered here 4,500 years ago to bury their dead, making this the oldest known cemetery in the United States. It is believed there were almost 200 burials in the area, although only 20 have been uncovered. Most were destroyed by modern gravel pit operations.

The Native Americans who lived here made tools of copper; interred and cremated their dead; and buried copper, stone, bone, and shell with them. The oldest forged implements in North America have been found there, and evidence of inhabitation goes back to 5600 B.C.E The Charles Werrebroeck Museum is at the site.

Located on Highway 22 at Highway 41,
2 miles west of Oconto, Oconto County.

Port des Morts

Today, Door County brings to mind beautiful images, but it got its name from "Port des Morts"—literally, "Death's Door." It was a place with frightening connotations for the Native Americans.

"Death's Door" derives its name from a legend about a war that was fought over the plenteous land near the head of the Green Bay peninsula. It's said a band of Potawatomi invaded the land of the Noquets, and war was declared. According to the legend, the warriors were struck by a breath of wind while on the water, and none returned alive. Many days later, the bodies washed up on the beach of Detroit Island.

Located at Gills Rock between the mainland and Washington Island, Door County.

Rock Island

Accessible only by ferryboat—no cars allowed—Rock Island was once home to Potawatomi, Huron, Petun, and Ottawa. Archeologists have found pottery, tools, and beads left behind. Ancient Indian village sites and burial sites are all well marked and legally protected.

Located northeast of Washington Island, Door County.

She-She-Pe-Ko-Naw (Chain O' Lakes)

John To-mow, who descended from the last great chief of the Menominee, described the Chain O' Lakes as "an Indian woman's string of beads which had become unfastened."

These beautiful clear lakes fed by the Crystal River are known for mounds and Native American trails, but few are open to the public. Near Rustic Roads 23 and 24, Pope Lake is an undeveloped lake in the chain with clear deep waters and many legends surrounding it.

Located on Highway 49 between Highways 54 and 22, just southwest of Waupaca, Waupaca County.

Taylor Lake Mound

Also known as Catfish Mound or Sanders Mound, this "catfish-shaped" mound was originally 250 feet long and almost 30 feet wide, but more than half was destroyed through cultivation. The horns of the catfish are 15 feet wide. A bronze tablet provided by the Monday Night Club in 1913 marks the mound.

Located just off Highway 22 on Taylor Lake, southwest of Waupaca, Waupaca County.

Taylor Lake Mound, Waupaca

Whispering Pines Spirit Stone

Whispering Pines Park features many paths, springs, and strange rock and wood formations; a large granite boulder near an old Indian trail is believed to have been a Native American Manitou shrine or spirit stone. A plaque at the entrance of the park reads, "The things we love are most precious when we share them with others."

Located on Marl Lake, on the western end of the
Chain O' Lakes, Waupaca County.

Potawatomi Indian Reservation

The Potawatomi Reservation is home to about half of the 980 tribal members and encompasses about 12,000 acres. The Potawatomi (Bode Wad Mi) are named "Keepers of the Fire" for the task of keeping the sacred fire as part of the Confederacy of the Ojibwe (Chippewa) and Ottawa. The headquarters is located in Crandon.

Indian Springs, a large natural springs in the area, is considered sacred and is on protected land. It feeds several trout streams in Forest County. The Potawatomi named their 99-room hotel Indian Springs Lodge. Sugar Bush Hill, near Crandon on reservation land, is also sacred. As the second-highest point in Wisconsin (1,950 feet), it provides a wonderful panoramic view of surrounding forests and lakes.

Located on Highway 8, east of Crandon, Forest County.
Tribal offices: (800) 777-1640 or (715) 478-2903.

Wabeno

The community of Wabeno (meaning "wise" or "mysterious" men) was named for the fourth-degree title in the Medicine Lodge (Medewin) Society. Located on Highway 32, Forest County.

Menominee Indian Reservation

The word *menominee* means "people of the wild rice." The peace-loving Menominee, also known as the Algonquians, are Wisconsin's oldest continuing residents, surviving more than 10,000 years in the area. They call themselves "Kiash Matchitiwuk"—the Ancient Ones. In 1852, the tribe moved up the Wolf River and, by 1854, they were in 10 townships. Today the reservation contains 235,000 acres of forestland, and about 5,500 people live there. Their creation stories lead them to the mouth of the Menominee River, 60 miles east of the current reservation, where the five clans—ancestral Bear, Eagle, Wolf, Moose, and Crane—were created.

Located at Highways 49 and 55, 5 miles north of Shawano, Menominee County, (715) 799-5114.

Also known as Our Lady of the Woods, the **Ka-no-po-way Church and Cemetery** site features an old Indian cemetery with headstones for many members of the Menominee tribe.

Located 7 miles northeast of the village of Keshena, Menominee County.

Jebaiesa Supet, the Menominee name for the group of effigy mounds on the east bank of the Wolf River, means "where the little corpse lies." This site is not accessible to the public, but there is a spot to pull over on the road and look out on the beautiful Wolf River. It is very likely that the mounds were here before the reservation because the Menominee people often were enemies of the mound builders.

Located on Highway 55 at Five Islands, on the Menominee Indian Reservation, Menominee County.

Spirit Rock

According to Menominee legend, a warrior once asked a god for eternal life. The request angered the god, who turned the warrior into a rock—making his wish come true in that the rock would be "everlasting." At night, kindly spirits lay offerings of tobacco on the rock, which is now known as Spirit Rock. Eventually, it's said, the rock will crumble, and when it does, the Menominee race will disappear with it. The stone is located just off the road and is marked by a public marker.

Located on Highway 55, 4 miles north of Keshena, Menominee County.

Spirit Rock, near Keshena

Sakaogon (Mole Lake) Indian Reservation

Sakaogon, called Mole Lake, is one of six Ojibwe tribal bands in Wisconsin. Tribal headquarters are in Crandon. The reserve is on about 2,000 acres in Forest County.

Mole Lake Burial Mound is the site of a major battle between the Sioux and the Ojibwe in 1806. More than 500 Ojibwe and Sioux were killed and buried in a common mound. The tribes fought over control of wild rice beds; the Sioux never returned to the site. Today it's a wooded wayside.

*Located on Highway 55, north of Mole Lake,
Forest County, (715) 478-2604.*

Oneida Reservation

The Oneida Tribe is a member of the Iroquois Confederacy, going back to the 1500s. As a result of land deals made in the east, many Oneidas relocated here, settling along the Duck Creek—10 miles outside of the city of Green Bay. Today the reserve is about 5,000 acres, with about 4,500 tribal members. The Oneida Nation Museum has one of the largest ongoing exhibitions of Oneida Indian history, including an authentic bark longhouse and other hands-on exhibits.

Cornelius Hill, "last chief and first priest of the Oneidas" (1834–1907), is buried in the **Holy Apostles Episcopal Church and Cemetery (Oneida Indian Mission)**. The church's first sermon was preached in a log chapel in 1825 in what was originally called the Hobart Church. The current church building dates back to 1886. As early as 1821, its hymnal was printed in phonetic sounds so the natives could read it in their own language.

Located at 2937 Freedom Road, Oneida, Brown County, (920) 869-2565.

Stockbridge-Munsee Mohican

The Stockbridge-Munsee band of Mohican Indians is originally from the New York State area, having relocated here in the 1800s. In 1856, they finally settled in treaty land in Shawano County. The current reservation is about 16,000 acres in trust lands. The tribe claims about 1,400 members in and around the reservation. Tribal headquarters are located in Shawano: (715) 793-4111.

Before settling farther north, the tribal band had a thriving community around Stockbridge. The small **Stockbridge Indian Cemetery** commemorates not only the tribal people but also other 19th-century settlers. The cemetery is on the National Register of Historic Places.

Located off Highway 55 at Moore Road, Stockbridge, Calumet County.

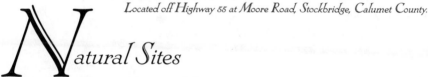

Natural Sites

Ridges Sanctuary and Park

This private nonprofit wildflower preserve is home to some of the rarest wildflowers in North America. There is a small fee to enter. A sign at one of the entrance areas requests that visitors observe silence to keep the space meditative.

Baileys Harbor Ridges Park is the adjacent county park that includes a 400-foot sand beach and two historic lighthouses. The ridges are named for actual ridges formed as the countryside rebounded from the Ice Age.

Located on County Q at Highway 57, northeast of Baileys Harbor, Door County.
Baileys Harbor Ridges Park is located half a mile down Ridges Road
off Highway 57. Contact Door County Parks: (920) 746-9959.

Monument Point

This beautiful rock formation is on the Green Bay side of the peninsula.

Located on County B (Monument Point Road), south of
Horseshoe Bay, Egg Harbor, Door County.

Cathedral of Pines

For all those people who say they don't need to step into a church because they feel closer to God in the woods, this area of the Nicolet National Forest illustrates what they're talking about. According to legend, these now-400-year-old pines were saved from the logging saw due to the pleadings of the wife of the logging company. This small area is all that remains of Oconto County's virgin pines. A couple of rustic benches are provided for resting and meditating beneath the trees that seem to reach all the way up to the sky.

Located between Archibald Lake and Little Archibald Lake, Nicolet National Forest, Oconto County. From Highway 32, turn west on Archibald Lake Road and right on Cathedral Drive, (920) 485-2942 or (920) 485-4663.

Cave Point County Park

Surrounded by Whitefish Dunes State Park, the limestone sea caves provide an unforgettable sight and sound as the waters of Lake Michigan crash here. Caves are formed by carbonic acid in the water. The Sevastopol Sand Dunes are nearby, forming a magnificent beach area (although the water is usually too cold for swimming).

Located in Whitefish Dunes State Park on Lake Michigan, eastern Door County. Take County WD from Highway 57 to the park and follow the signs to Cave Point. Door County Parks: (920) 746-9959.

Catholic Sites
Wisconsin's Holy Land

More than a dozen Catholic churches (and towns named after them) are gathered within a 15-mile radius in Fond du Lac County, in the heart of what's called "Wisconsin's Holy Land." European Catholics settled this heavily Catholic area. Today, with the shortage of priests an issue, many of the churches are working to merge congregations. These are some of the churches in the area.

St. Patrick's, 41 W. Follette; **St. Mary's**, 93 Marquette Street; and **St. Louis**, 209 N. Macy Street, are all in the city of Fond du Lac. **St. John the Baptist**, on the National Register of Historic Places, is at County Q and County W in Johnsburg. St. Catherine's Bay, the site of a forgotten village laid out in 1852 and later destroyed by floods, once included St. Catherine's Church, named for St. Catherine of Siena. The area is located at the east shore of Lake Winnebago in Calumet County. **St Peter's**, which features the Our Lady of Fatima Grotto dating back to 1915, is in the community of St. Peter, about 8 miles northeast of Fond du Lac. **St. Mary's Springs** features several wonderful statues, including a guardian angel with child and a grotto of St. Joseph. One of the former school buildings was built around the turn of the century. A natural spring runs through the property. It is located on Highway 23 on the edge of Fond du Lac. **St. Martin's** dates back to 1847 and is located on Highway 67 in Ashford. **St. Claudius,** dating back to 1905, features a grotto to the Virgin Mary. St. Claudius School, dating to 1911, is right next door, at County G and County C north of Highway 23, St. Cloud. Another **St. John the Baptist,** built in 1862, featuring beautiful stained glass of blue and purple flower patterns, is located on County B, east of Sherwood in St. John.

Chapel at St. John the Baptist Catholic Church, Johnsburg

In the center of the Holy Land is the town of Mount Calvary. In 1846, Father Caspar Rehrl built a log church on the hill that overlooks the entire area. In 1853, Bishop Martin Henni of Milwaukee named the chapel Holy Cross on Calvary Church because it was set on a hill; he named the town Mount Calvary in honor of the hill where Jesus Christ was crucified.

In town, **St. Lawrence Seminary** (and Friary), founded in 1857, features many inspirational statues (including 14 Stations of the Cross going down the hillside cemetery), St. Joseph's chapel (circa 1872), and a stunning relief mural of different moments of St. Francis of Assisi's life. The seminary is located on College Avenue (at Highway 149 and County W) in Mount Calvary.

St. Nazianz

In 1854, German Father Ambrose Oschwald bought land in Manitowoc County to found a Catholic village, an experimental community he called "Das Settlement." He built two log houses and the church, **St. Gregory Nazianz**, in 1864. Damaged by windstorms in the spring of 2000—along with most of the other buildings in St. Nazianz—the structure has been repaired and rededicated. St. Gregory is on the National Register of Historic Places and is located at 212 Church Street, (920) 773-2511.

The village was the home of the former **St. Nazianz Seminary**. Now closed, the seminary is also on the National Register of Historic Places and is right next to the church.

Nearby, the **Loretto Shrine** is a humble little chapel on a high hill overlooking St. Nazianz, built in 1870. Rededicated in 1979 in memory of Brother Bordin Junwirth (1895–1979), the chapel was part of the first permanent community of the Salvadorian Brothers in the United States. The shrine is on the National Register of Historic Places. Drive through the abandoned seminary grounds to the shrine, which can be found behind a small graveyard of Salvadorians. It is located at the intersection of County A and County U, just south of St. Nazianz.

St. Mary's Convent was home to the Sisters of the Divine Savior from 1888 to 1988 and is now an independent convent. The building is set on beautiful wooded acreage beside Lake Oschwald that includes a small vineyard. Located at 300 S. Second Avenue, (920) 773-2515.

The **Lax Chapel,** for which the beautiful rural road that runs from the Sheboygan River near Kiel to St. Nazianz was named, is a wooden Catholic church —rustic, rural, and romantic. It is used primarily for weddings and is open for an annual Mass celebrated by the pastor of St. Gregory's in St. Nazianz. For more information, contact St. Gregory's.

Father Allouez Sites

Father Claude-Jean Allouez was ordained at the Society of Jesus at Toulouse in 1655 and set out for Quebec in 1658. He's been called the founder of Catholicism in the West. Allouez traveled extensively in the New World, forming missions—predominantly in the area that would later become Wisconsin, and especially in what is now the Green Bay area.

A statue entitled *The Spirit of the Northwest* was erected in Father Allouez's honor at Courthouse Square on Walnut Street in Green Bay. It was created in 1912 by Sydney Bedore.

St. Francis Xavier Cathedral is spiritually connected to the early missionaries and is located at 139 S. Madison, Green Bay, Brown County, (920) 432-

4348. gbdioc.org/parishes/green_bay_downtown.htm

The first Catholic cemetery in Wisconsin (now known as **Allouez Catholic Cemetery and Chapel**) was established in 1822 and is located at 2121 Riverside, Allouez, Brown County, (920) 435-6850.

St. Francis Xavier Grotto was dedicated in 1935 by Father Gloudemans and located off Highway 57, Brussels, Door County.

Cross marking the site of St. Francis Xavier Mission, Oconto

A rugged cross on the Oconto River marks the site of the first Catholic mission in northeast Wisconsin, the **Mission of St. Francis Xavier**. There was a primitive chapel at the site, and 600 Native Americans attended services there. The area is now a campground. Located between Chicago and Main Streets on Brazeau Avenue, Oconto, Oconto County.

Old St. Joseph Church

Fostered by the Norbertine fathers, St. Norbert College began when Father Bernard Henry Pennings taught Frank Van Dyke his first Latin lesson there in October 1898. Pennings and his fellow Sons of St. Norbert, from Berne Abby in Holland, were installed there in 1898.

According to legend, the century-old St. Joseph's Church was built on the same site as a mission built in 1676 by Father Alabanel. The parish was established 200 years later. Starting in 1998, Old St. Joseph's was completely gutted and totally refurbished; the rededication service was held on March 19, 1999.

Pews have been replaced with chairs so concerts can be held there, and new artwork and a new organ were installed. The $3.2 million project has won an award from the Interfaith Forum for Religious Architecture, as well as the Eugene Potene Liturgical Design Award.

See also St. Norbert Abbey, under Church Camps and Retreat Centers, later in this chapter.

Located at 100 Grant Street, DePere, Brown County, (920) 337-3181.

St. John the Baptist Church (Egg Harbor)

Constructed of beautiful multicolored stones, this church combines native quarried stone with indigenous rocks found as glacier erratics in Door County. It is a familiar landmark on a drive through Egg Harbor.

Located on County G, Egg Harbor, Door County, (920) 868-2410.
gbdioc.org/parishes/egg_harbor.htm

St. John Baptist Church (Montello)

A church building used to sit on top of protruding granite that was mined during the city's quarry days. Montello Granite, uniquely purplish-red in color, has been used on monuments nationally, including Grant's Tomb in New York City. In the center of the city is a beautiful park where the quarry used to be. Springwater now fills the 150-foot holes left from the granite mining. In 1992, Irv Daggett deeded the water-filled quarry to the city of Montello. There are five constructed waterfalls in all on the 10-acre parcel park development, which includes a nativity scene at Christmastime and a small church that regularly plays religious music. One of the waterfalls is 40 feet tall. White swans glide on the water beneath the miniature church.

Located on Montello Street (Highway 23),
Montello, Marquette County.

Chapel of Our Lady of Good Help

Located at a site where multiple miracles occurred dating back to the 1800s, the chapel is said to be where an apparition of the Blessed Virgin Mary appeared to a young girl, Adele Brisse. She became a nun and started a small order at the chapel. Now, the chapel is cared for by the Discalced Carmelite Nuns who live near the chapel, even though the order is not connected to the shrine. It is also known as the Robinsonville Chapel after the rural township at the eastern edge of the county where it is located.

*Located at 4047 Chapel Drive, New Franken,
Brown County, (920) 866-2571.*

Shrine of the Blessed Virgin Mary

Next to the old St. Anthony's Church building is what has been called "one of the finest shrines to the Blessed Virgin" in the upper Midwest. The new and modern St. Anthony's has a beautiful gray granite altar that is made of 4.5 tons of rock.

*Located at 1432 River Street (Highway 141), Niagara, Marinette County,
on the border with Michigan's Upper Peninsula.*

Church of the Assumption of the Blessed Virgin Mary

This breathtaking church dates back to 1886. With its huge and magnificent main chapel, seven rose windows, and ornate design, it's the kind of church you would expect to see in a large urban area.

*Located at 124 E. Pulaski Street (Highway 32 at Highway 160),
Pulaski, Brown County, (920) 822-3279. abvm.org*

Julieski Millennium Shrine

Central Wisconsin is full of little roadside crosses and shrines, like the Julieski roadside shrine, which sits across the road from the Polish National Cemetery. The Julieski shrine was dedicated in 1901 and has been rededicated recently According to tradition, these roadside shrines are dedicated and erected at each century mark. The shrines represent a fusion between Christian and pre-Christian understandings of specific locations. For example, these grottos are often found at intersections—a place where pagans believed demons would hide. Most of the roadside shrines exist in Polish areas of Wisconsin.

Located on Highway 32 at County S, north of Pulaski, Oconto County.

St. Mary Church

This picturesque, German Gothic church can be seen from Smith Park on Doty Island. With its exquisite wood-carved side and front altars and painted Stations of the Cross, the building was built in 1883 to replace the former building that had burned down on Ash Wednesday of the same year.

A large sacristy was added to it later, as was an 18-classroom school. The present-day rectory was built in 1936 under Father John Hummel, who also enlarged the grounds and completed the auditorium. The new altar, facing the people, was erected in response to Vatican II. The building has seen a number of improvements and renovations over the years.

Located at 212 Appleton Street, Menasha, Winnebago County, (920) 725-7714.

St. Agnes Episcopal Church, Kewaunee

*E*piscopal Sites

St. Agnes Episcopal Church

Formerly known as Grace Church, the building overlooking Lake Michigan was erected in 1877, making it one of the oldest churches in Kewaunee County. It was a brick veneer interpretation of the plan for a board and batten church in the book *Rural Architecture*, published in 1852. The book's author, Richard Upjohn, was a founding member of the American Institute of Architects and was the designer of Wall Street's Trinity Church. The church burned in 1884 and was rebuilt, following the original plan, in 1891. Upjohn designed this building according to church publications. It is part of the city's historic walking tour. The interior has beautiful stained glass and woodwork, and when the door is open, there is a spectacular view of Lake Michigan.

Located at 806 Fourth Street (also 1226 Lake Street), Algoma, Kewaunee County, (920) 487-5677.

Cathedral Church of St. Paul

This congregation of St. Paul's dates back to 1875. The church features a magnificent collection of nearly 40 German wood carvings.

Located at 51 W. Division Street, Fond du Lac, Fond du Lac County,
(800) 937-9123 or (920) 921-3363.

Convent of the Holy Nativity Episcopal Church

Built in 1899 and operated by the Order of Sisters of the Holy Nativity, this Gothic Revival-style convent offers 40 retreat rooms. Private retreats are available for a few days for a freewill offering. Write in advance for information and to make a reservation.

Located at 101 E. Division Street, Fond du Lac,
Fond du Lac County, (920) 921-3363.

Christ Episcopal Church

The oldest Episcopal parish in Wisconsin and the oldest church in Green Bay, Christ Church was founded in 1826. At the time, Wisconsin was part of the territory of Michigan, and Green Bay was a small settlement called Navarino. In the mid-1830s, a church building was built using monies earned at a church benefit sale. The original building was a small, modified colonial frame building.

After the wood church burned down on July 3, 1898, in what was thought to be arson, a new building was erected about a year later. A seven-foot crucifix carved by a group of German craftsmen was given to the church in 1920 and now sits on the beam that separates the nave from the sanctuary. The new school and sacristy were built in 1956. The interior of the "Mother Church of the Northwest" was renovated in 1972.

Located at 425 Cherry Street, Green Bay, Brown County,
(920) 432-0042.

St. Peter's Episcopal Church

St. Peter's began its long history as Grace Church; its cornerstone was laid and the church was consecrated in January 1861. The building features a steep roof, an unusual rose window with a passionflower design, and an English pipe organ. Thirteen stained glass windows depict the life of the apostle Peter, the church's patron saint. The name of the church was changed to St. Peter's in

1866 to correspond to the church in Ripon, Yorkshire, England, for which the community was named. It's on the National Register of Historic Places.

Located at 217 Houston Street, Ripon,
Fond du Lac County, (920) 748-2422.

Our Lady of Walsingham Shrine at Grace Episcopal Church

A most unusual feature of Grace Church is the Shrine to Our Lady of Walsingham, erected in 1931. In the United States, Episcopal shrines are uncommon. Pilgrims from around the United States and England come to the shrine in May and October. The statue of the Virgin Mary and the Holy Child in the shrine is an exact replica of the statue in the shrine at Walsingham, in Norfolk, England, which dates back to 1061. A daily shrine service is held at 5:30 p.m.

Grace Church held its first service at Christmas 1847. It is the oldest church in Sheboygan to be on the same site continuously. The existing "Country Gothic" building was erected in 1870. The chapel is very "high church," similar to DeKoven's chapel in southeastern Wisconsin, but without the antiphonal seating.

Located at 1011 N. Seventh Street, Sheboygan,
Sheboygan County, (920) 452-9659.

St. Mary's Chapel

As a mission of St. Peter's Episcopal Church in Ripon, St. Mary's holds services every Saturday evening at 6:30 p.m. and on special days. A small rustic chapel in the pines at Bugh's Lake, St. Mary's was built according to a promise made by builder John Barnes in 1932—in memory of his parents and in thanksgiving for his surviving the sinking of the English ship *Tuscania.* All the stones were hand set by Barnes. There is a grotto for Mary and a carved-stone crucifix. In 1936, more than 3,000 people visited the tiny chapel. The total capacity is only 25. It is normally locked during the week but can be visited by appointment.

Located at Bugh's Lake, Highway 21, east of Wautoma,
Waushara County, (920) 293-4978. You can also call
St Peter's Episcopal Church (listed previously).

Methodist Sites

Smithfield Church Site

The first Methodist congregation in the region, dating back to 1830, was in a former Oneida Indian village, once called Smithfield and now part of Kimberly. On a Kimberly bluff overlooking the Fox River, two large cedars mark what can be called a sacred shrine to Methodists of Wisconsin.

Located along Highway 96, in Kimberly, Outagamie County.

Greenville Church

The first Evangelical Association Church was built in 1844. Eventually, the association became an integral part of the movement toward what would become the United Methodist Church. It is located on the other side of Appleton from the Smithfield site (previous listing). The present building houses the Wisconsin United Methodist Church Museum.

*Located at N1966 Julian Drive (Highway 45 at Highway 76),
Greenville, Outagamie County, (920) 757-5101.*

Lawrence Memorial Chapel

The Wisconsin Conference of the United Methodist Church was born here in 1969. The 1,248-seat auditorium chapel was built in 1919 and renovated in 1993. It features a 41-stop mechanical action organ. While Methodists helped with the founding of Lawrence University, it is now a private liberal arts college.

*Located at Lawrence University, 115 S. Drew Street, Appleton,
Outagamie County, (920) 832-7000.*

Rock Hill Chapel and Cemetery

"The Little Welsh Church" was the product of a Welsh Methodist settlement around Mt. Morian. The building was used for "Gymanfu Ganu" (service in song), an annual event, which was restarted in 1951. The adjacent cemetery includes some unique headstones shaped like trees and some Welsh headstones that date back to the 1850s. The church building is no longer in regular use.

*Located a half mile northeast of the town of Dalton on County H,
off Highway 44, Green Lake County.*

"The Little Wesh Church," Dalton

Algoma Boulevard Methodist Church & Nativity Museum

Built in 1874, this church building features a unique nativity collection with more than 600 nativity sets of glass, stone, paper, needlepoint—you name it. This is a wonderful thing for the kids to see—any time of the year, but especially around Christmas. (Of course, "kids" can be of any age.) The nativity sets come from around the world and are both ancient and modern. Donations are welcome. The collection is in the lower level of the building and is open during regular church hours and for groups by appointment. The church is listed on the National Register of Historic Places and is near the Paine Art Center and the Oshkosh Public Museum.

Located at 1174 Algoma Boulevard (at New York Avenue),
Oshkosh, Winnebago County, (920) 231-2800.

Stavkirke

Stavkirke (Norwegian for "mast church") follows an architectural style that dates back to the end of the 11th century, during the reign of St. Olav of Norway. At that time, Christian beliefs were just being introduced to Scandinavia, and the unique architecture blended ancient Norse tradition with the new ways of worship. Stavkirke architectural design is also known for dragon-scale shingles and carved dragon heads at roof peaks, there to scare away evil spirits. Other carved protector animals, such as deer, birds, and fish, may be seen along with stylized crosses.

There are several examples of the stavkirke in Wisconsin, most notably in Door County. The finest example of a stavkirke in the area can be found on Washington Island, which was settled by Swedish and Icelandic peoples. "Attracted by the similarity to the rugged beauty and rockbound coastlines of their homelands, fishermen, sailors, and craftsmen settled this windswept island," says a brochure for the island's stavkirke. "What more perfect way to pay tribute to this heritage than to build an authentic stave church, to serve as a quiet reminder of the men and women who brought their faith across the ocean and carved out a living in the New World."

To get to the church, follow the "prayer path," a beautiful little walk through the woods, and you come across a stunning structure made of cedar and formed after a Viking ship. Although regular services are not held there, the stavkirke provides a place for small worship services, gatherings, and weddings. It helps serve the ministry of Trinity Evangelical Lutheran Church.

Located on Washington Island, Door County.

Stavkirke on Washington Island

Just south of Baileys Harbor and also in Door County is the **Bjorklunden Chapel**, a replica of a 15th-century Norwegian stavkirke, built between 1939 and 1947. Also known as the Boynton Chapel, it is filled with intricate Scandinavian symbols lovingly carved and a mural of the Angels of Prayer. Tours are available mid-June through Labor Day, Mondays and Wednesdays from 1 to 4 p.m.

Located at 7603 Chapel Lane, Baileys Harbor, (920) 839-2216. Take Highway 57 about 4.5 miles north of Jacksonport. Look for Anchutz Plumbing and turn at the driveway across the road; look for signs for Lawrence University and then follow signs for the chapel.

In Egg Harbor, alongside an antique shop is an example of a building that could have been used for pagan worship and features ornate carvings and hand-painted murals. This tiny building is surrounded by a wonderful garden.

Located beside Orchard View Resale and Antique Barn, County EE and Highway 42, Egg Harbor.

Little Norway, a valley west of Mount Horeb in southwestern Wisconsin, is home to another example of unique stavkirke architecture. Little Norway is also known as Nissedahle or Valley of the Elves. Built in Norway in a 12th-century style, the stavkirke here was originally part of the 1893 Columbian Exposition in Chicago. No services are held, but a tour is available, and a museum is open from May through October.

Located off Highway 18/151, 3 miles west of Mount Horeb in Dane County. Take the Cave of the Mounds Road exit, (608) 437-8211.

Lutheran Sites

Lutheran Indian Mission

The Rev. Jeremiah Slingerland, tribal member, pastor, and teacher, taught Mohican children at this Lutheran mission school. Hundreds of Native American children were educated there between 1908 and 1958. The dormitory building, still standing, was erected in 1921. The Stockbridge-Munsee Mohican Tribe derived spiritual and academic education there until it closed in 1958. The buildings are on the National Register of Historic Places.

Located on County G north of Upper Red Lake, Shawano County.

St. Paul's Evangelical Lutheran Church

One of the only log churches in the country still used for regular services, the building is more than 50 years old. Affiliated with the Wisconsin Evangelical Lutheran Synod, the pastor actually travels to the log chapel from the Michigan Peninsula.

Located 1 block south of Highway 70, Tipler,
Florence County, (906) 265-6662.

Other Christian Sites

Ephraim Church of the Brotherhood (Moravian)

The Moravian Church is one of the few Protestant churches that predates Martin Luther's 1517 thesis against the Catholic Church. Starting in Moravia and Bohemia, Moravians—then known as the Hussites—were persecuted for 40 years. Today, the Moravians' guiding principle is, "In essentials unity, in non-essentials liberty, and in all things love."

A group of 40 Norwegian Moravians settled in Door County in 1853. They named the area Ephraim, a biblical term that means "doubly fruitful." This simple but elegant wood structure overlooks Green Bay (the building was moved from the shore to the hill in 1883) and is the oldest church building on the Door County peninsula. A total of 130 attended the church's first service held in December 1859, arriving by foot and sleigh. The building, which is on the National Register of Historic Places, was remodeled in 1916 and again in the early 1950s.

Located at 9970 Moravian Street, Ephraim, Door County, (920) 854-2804.

First Church of Christ, Scientist

This building, completed in 1886, was the first building erected solely for Christian Science worship. Mary Baker Eddy had founded the Church of Christ, Scientist seven years earlier in Boston. After a spontaneous recovery from illness, Eddy devoted herself to the belief that truth is the only remedy to sin and sickness and that healing comes directly from God and not from doctors. Still in regular use, the building is on the National Register of Historic Places.

Located at Chicago and Main Streets,
Oconto, Oconto County.

First Church of Christ, Scientist, Oconto

First Dutch Reformed Church

This is the oldest Reformed church in Wisconsin, dating back to 1850 and founded by Dutch immigrants to the area. There were about 60 Dutch families in Sheboygan County by 1849. The church moved three times before it came to rest in its current location. In 1987, a fire gutted the church. By 1989, the congregation dedicated a new sanctuary and an education wing.

Located at 927 Superior Avenue, Oostburg, Sheboygan County.
Take exit 116 off I-43 into Oostburg; this turns into Center Avenue.
Turn left on South Ninth Street. Superior Avenue is one block down,
(920) 564-2319.

First Congregational Church of Ripon

Founded in 1850, First Congregational Church is the oldest continuous church organization in Ripon. Its original meetinghouse was the first church to be built in the area. Founded by members of the Wisconsin Phalanx, an experimental community founded on the principles of French philosopher Charles Fourier, the congregation passed resolutions against slavery early on and looked kindly upon the leadership of women.

The first of the Bovay Meetings, which led to the formation of the Republican Party, were held in this church in 1854. The church's architect, Edward Townsend Mix, was the State Architect for Wisconsin. The front entrance features a Romanesque arch detail, and a distinctive detailed metal cross tops the church spire and clock tower. The building, next to Ripon College, is on the National Register of Historic Places. See also Ceresco Park under "Other Sites," later in this chapter.

Located at 220 Ranson Street, Ripon,
Fond du Lac County, (920) 748-5898.

St. Spyridon Greek Orthodox Church

Built in 1906, this is one of the oldest Greek Orthodox churches in Wisconsin, and it is one of the oldest Eastern Orthodox churches of any jurisdiction in the state. Stained glass icons are visible from outside.

Located at 1427 S. 10th Street, Sheboygan,
Sheboygan County, (920) 452-3096.

St. Hubert Shrine

You have to drive almost seven miles down a rustic dirt road and may think you'll never get there, but be patient. St. Hubert Shrine, located in a beautiful clearing by the water, is worth the drive. This little clearing in the woods by a rustling creek is an isolated place for meditation, and it includes a picnic shelter. A unique feature is a sign with "The Prayer of the Woods," reading, in part: "I am the bread of kindness and the flower of beauty; ye who pass by, listen to my prayer: harm me not."

Located on Shrine Goodman Road, 1 mile east and 6.8 miles
north of Goodman, Marinette County.

Friends Church—"Old Rugged Cross"

"On a hill far away stood an old rugged cross / The emblem of suffering and shame / And I love that old cross where the dearest and best / For a world of lost sinners was slain. . . ." A historical marker at the Friends Church here marks the place where composer George Bennard introduced this hymn. The hymn was first sung from penciled words and notes as a quartet, then as a duet at the church's last service on January 12, 1913. The Gothic Revival church itself is historic, dating back to 1885.

Located at 204 W. Maple Street, Sturgeon Bay,
Door County, (920) 743-2714.

Waba Nun Nung Gospel Chapel

A small brick and wood building, Waba Nun Nung, or "Morning Star," Community Gospel Chapel is directly across the road from the Mole Lake Burial Mound Memorial. The nondistinct building is part of the Midwest Indian Mission, which started in Crandon in 1964. Behind the church is an old graveyard with many traditionally native graves as well as Christian markers.

Located on the Mole Lake Reservation on Highway 55,
Forest County, (715) 478-3385.

First Spiritualist's Society of Omro

This site once boasted the most important Spiritualistic center in Wisconsin. The center got its start in the 1860s. By 1877, a monument had been erected to the Society, and well-known Spiritualists traveled from all over the United States to Wisconsin to speak. Sixty children formed a special Sunday school called the Children's Progressive Lyceum, which still stands as a historic site. Studies were Spiritualistic but "instructed the children how to become upright and independent men and women."

The mysterious murder of a local farmer, John Sullivan, gave the mediums something to concentrate their energies on. But the mystery was never solved. The Society fell apart within a couple of decades due to infighting as well as criticism from other religious groups.

For more information, contact the Omro Historical Society, 144 E. Main Street,
Omro, Winnebago County, (920) 685-6123.

Jewish Sites

Temple Zion Synagogue

Now dilapidated, but still beautiful, this Victorian-style building was built in 1884 and used until 1978. Rabbi Samuel Weiss—magician Harry Houdini's father—helped the congregation build its first temple. Author Edna Ferber worshipped there. The building was built with financial support of many, including non-Jews. On the National Register of Historic Places, it now houses Wahl Organ Builders and is in the process of being renovated.

Located at 320 N. Durkee Street, Appleton, Outagamie County.

Jewish Sites in Northeastern Wisconsin

Although there have been Jewish communities in northeastern Wisconsin since the late 1800s, only a few synagogues and Jewish sites remain.

In the Sheboygan area, Ahavas Scholem Congregation merged with Adas Israel and formed **Beth El Congregation**, at 1007 North Avenue in Sheboygan, (920) 452-5828.

The **Sheboygan Hebrew Cemetery**, located in Kohler, is known for the unique and beautiful Hebrew headstones. The cemetery is on the National Register of Historic Places and has graves that date to the 1870s.

There are a couple of beautiful synagogues that are about 50 years old. **Anshe Poale Zedek** is located in the midst of a number of older churches, including Presbyterian and Episcopal. This Manitowoc synagogue was built in 1954; it is located at 435 N. Eighth Street, (920) 682-4511.

Congregation B'nai Israel, built in the same era, is located across the street from the Algoma Boulevard Methodist Church on Vine Street in Oshkosh, (920) 235-4270.

Other Sites

Ceresco Park

Founded in 1844, Wisconsin Phalanx was an experimental community run according to the teachings of Charles Fourier, a French social philosopher. A historic marker is placed at the site of the utopian community that preceded the 1854 birth of the Republican Party in Ripon. Warren Chase, a follower of Fourier, named the village for Ceres, the Roman Goddess of Agriculture. Behind the park is the main communal longhouse where many of the 200 community members shared their existence. It has been converted to apartments. Ceresco Valley became a part of Ripon in 1853.

Located at 26–34 Warren Street, Ripon, Fond du Lac County.

Pathways of Light

"With over 30 years of 'service to spiritual awakening,' the purpose of Pathways of Light is to provide a safe environment in which awareness of Inner Wisdom is nurtured," says their 1998 catalog. The facility provides ministerial and facilitator training, as well as some individual and family retreats. Workshops include "A Course in Miracles."

Located at 13111 Lax Chapel Road, Kiel,
Manitowoc County, (920) 894-2339.

Church Camps and Retreat Centers

Although retreat centers and religious camps are scattered throughout the state, the northeast region of Wisconsin seems to have a particularly large cluster of them. The following is not meant to be an exhaustive listing of retreat centers (neither is the appendix). It includes only those that are unique or historic in some way and have incorporated some elements of sacredness into their facilities or grounds.

Green Lake Conference Center (Baptist)

A visit to Green Lake Conference Center can last a day, a weekend, or longer. The Center features a wide variety of attractions for pilgrims.

The Center opened in 1944 and has a mission to "welcome all to a Christian environment of natural beauty, hospitality, and acceptance. Through experiences of training, worship, fellowship, and recreation, persons are refreshed, renewed, and transformed for their journey of life and service."

One unique feature of Green Lake is its observation towers. The main one, Judson Tower, provides a beautiful view (you can pick up a key at the administration office). The tower bears a cross that was presented by hundreds of Baptist youth in 1945 "in gratitude for these hallowed grounds and their meaning for generations to come." The tower was renovated in 1990.

Visiting "Grace," the chapel car, is a treat. The retired railroad car, dedicated in 1915, has been renovated and is permanently parked near the administration office (again, pick up a key). It was one of a fleet of seven railroad cars used to spread the gospel in the late 1800s and early 1900s. Each car contained a chapel area and living quarters for a traveling preacher. The car is available for small group meetings and Bible studies.

The Cathedral in the Glen is a replica of a woodland chapel built by Baptist missionaries who were martyred in 1943 in the Philippines. The Spurgeon chapel is dedicated to Charles Haddon Spurgeon, 1834–1892, the "Prince of Preachers," who is said to have preached to more than 60,000 people.

Green Lake offers a number of lodges and camping areas, as well as a wide variety of outdoor recreation options including swimming, golf, and winter sports.

Located at W 2511 Highway 23, Green Lake, Green Lake County, (920) 294-3323.
greenlake-aba.org/homepagenew.htm

Judson Tower at the Green Lake Conference Center, Green Lake

Holy Name Retreat House (Catholic)

Every retreat to Holy Name Retreat House begins and ends with the 45-minute trip across Green Bay on the boat *Quo Vadis* ("Wither goest thou?"). The Retreat House, founded in 1951, is on a 40-foot bluff over the bay.

Casual retreats are offered for men, women, couples, and seminarians; they can be based in recovery and healing and can be private, charismatic, and directed. Silent retreats are a cherished tradition there. "Time on the island provides the opportunity to be alone, to cleanse our mind, to heal our soul, to communicate with ourselves and God." There are no stores or transportation on the island. Advance registration is required. A schedule is available by contacting the retreat center. The Retreat House is open only from May through mid-September.

Located 7 miles offshore of Fish Creek, at 1825 Riverside Drive, Chambers Island, Door County, (920) 437-7531 and (920) 734-1112. Accessible only by boat.

Monte Alverno Retreat Center (Catholic)

The state's oldest retreat center that was originally built as a retreat center (in 1934), Monte Alverno stands on a hill overlooking the Fox River. Sponsored by the Capuchin Franciscan Friars, the Center is open to all people who are seeking God, spiritual growth, and religious experience. Men and women's retreats are offered. About 3,000 attend the workshops and retreats each year. Morning prayer, presentations, Eucharist, and a healing service are part of the schedule. Monte Alverno is referred to as "Appleton's best-kept secret."

Located at 1000 N. Ballard Road, Appleton, Outagamie County, (920) 733-8526.

St. Joseph's Retreat Center (Catholic)

Originally a novitiate for Sacred Heart brothers, the facility began as a retreat center in the mid-1970s. Individual and group as well as directed Christian retreats are available.

Located at 3035 O'Brien Road on Kangaroo Lake, Baileys Harbor, Door County, (920) 839-2391.

St. Norbert Abbey Ministry & Life Center (Catholic)

The Norbertine Center for Spirituality features guided retreats and workshops, a labyrinth, and the National Shrine of St. Joseph, which is located under the Abbey church. The statue of St. Joseph was crowned by Bishop Messmer as a sequel to the approval of the Archconfraternity by Pope Leo XIII in 1892, and it is near the remains of Abbot Bernard Pennings and a display of memorabilia.

The Center offers 55 private, furnished bedrooms, six meeting rooms, a cloister garden, a bookstore, communal morning and evening prayers, and daily Mass with the Norbertines.

About 100 Norbertines live on-site, and work in pastoral ministry, education, foreign missions, social work, art, music, medicine, and hospital chaplaincies. The Norbertine Order is among the oldest orders in the Church, dating back almost 900 years.

The Norbertines' mission statement is as follows: "Christ and the Church call us to live as a community of one heart and one mind on the way to God, faithful to the gospel and our religious heritage, by our witness, our worship, our word, and our work, with emphasis on the contemporary needs of the Church and the poor."

Located south of the Fox River at 1016 N. Broadway (Highway 57),
DePere, Brown County, (920) 337-4315.

Camp Webb (Episcopal)

Owned by the diocese of Milwaukee, camp cabins feature biblical and religious names such as Aquinas, Antioch, Jerusalem, Nazareth, Gethsemane, etc. The camp is nestled in the beautiful woods on Hills Lake.

Located at N1875-21st Avenue, just off Highway 21, 5 miles east of Wautoma,
Washara County, (920) 787-3812.

Lucerne Camp and Retreat Center (Methodist)

Since its opening in 1947, Lucerne Camp and Retreat Center has been available for retreats, camps, and conferences. It now has 6,500 guests each year.

According to its mission statement, the camp affirms the mission of the Board of Camp and Retreat Ministries of the Wisconsin United Methodist Church "to provide settings for all ages to experience and appreciate the natural beauty of God's creation and enhance spiritual growth." The camp's primary focus is to be a provider for United Methodist groups and individuals, but "recognizing that we are all members of God, our additional focus is to be a provider for other not-for-profit organizations."

The camp features 48 beds and has meals available as group size allows. Group size is 5 to 50.

Located at County YY off Highway 73, between Wautoma and Neshkoro,
on Lake Lucerne, Waushara County, (920) 293-4488.

Mt. Morris Camp & Conference Center (Moravian)

Situated on a bluff with a beautiful view, this primitive camp is run by the western district of the Moravian Church. The area includes tepees, a winter lodge, and ice-skating in the winter. One of Rev. James Hicks's hand-built lodges is on the bluff overlooking the stream. As he said, "God has spoken to many in this spot."

Located on Blackhawk Road, off Highway 152, Mt. Morris, Waushara County, (608) 837-0537.

Northwest

Northwest Wisconsin

Including the counties of Ashland, Barron, Bayfield, Buffalo, Burnett, Chippewa, Clark, Douglas, Dunn, Eau Claire, Iron, Jackson, Lincoln, Marathon, Oneida, Pepin, Pierce, Polk, Portage, Price, Rusk, Sawyer, St. Croix, Taylor, Trempealeau, Vilas, Washburn, and Wood

Chapter *4*

Northwest
Wisconsin

C

ertain places in the natural world still possess a strange, perhaps
spiritual, charge, which we can sense almost immediately.

—Jane Hope, *The Secret Language of the Soul*

WISCONSIN'S NORTHWEST region, long held sacred by the Ojibwe, attract-ed Jesuit missionaries who erected the first Christian chapel in the state on Madeline Island. Before long, both Catholics and Protestants were well repre-sented in the area, both providing mission services to Native Americans.

The area has remained spiritually significant to the Native Americans, espe-cially Ojibwe (Chippewa) and Ho-Chunk (Winnebago), even as people of other faith traditions populated the area. The Native Americans both embraced Christianity and maintained their own spiritual traditions, sometimes merging the two. Visitors to many Native American sites, especially the Indian Village at Wa-Swa-Goning, can experience the ancient beliefs and traditions.

The immigration of Slavic peoples brought a different form of Christianity, Eastern Orthodoxy, to the region around the turn of the century. These people had fled religious persecution in their own countries, where atheistic govern-ments attempted to squelch religious expression. A century later, in the 1990s, the existence of a statue of Jesus in Marshfield sparked controversy when it was charged that the statue violated the separation of church and state.

Headwaters of the Wisconsin River at Lac Vieux Desert

*F*avorite *Sites*

- ɔ **Apostle Islands, Lake Superior**
  (nature, history, and spirits meet here)

- ɔ **Boulder Effigy Mound, Hager City**
  (another Wisconsin mystery)

- ɔ **Copper Falls State Park, Mellen**
  (breathtaking and inspirational waterfalls)

- ɔ **Dove Effigy Peace Mound, Neillsville**
  (modern effigy mound built for peace)

- ɔ **Holy Island, Washburn County**
  (a former retreat for clergy)

- ɔ **Holy Trinity Orthodox Church, Clayton**
  (an onion dome and Russian cross)

- ɔ **La Pointe du Saint Espirit, Madeline Island**
  (Wisconsin's oldest settlement)

- ɔ **La Pointe Indian Cemetery, Madeline Island**
  (sacred, protected, and traditional)

- ɔ **Old Man of the Dalles, Interstate State Park, St. Croix Falls**
  (he looks out over the water as a guardian)

- ɔ **Rice Lake Mounds, Rice Lake**
  (effigy mounds in a beautiful lakeside park)

- ɔ **St. Ann's Church and Cemetery, Rib Lake**
  (bells named Anna, Mary Theresa, and Elizabeth)

- ɔ **St. Clare Center for Spirituality, Custer**
  (a most lovely chapel)

- ɔ **St. Mary's Orthodox Church, Cornucopia**
  (a serene spot at the edge of the woods)

- ɔ **Wisconsin River Headwaters, Land O' Lakes**
  (where the waters begin)

- ɔ **Wa-Swa-Goning, Lac du Flambeau**
  (an authentic Indian village)

Apostle Islands

There are 22 Apostle Islands-but there were only 12 Apostles. Seventeenth-century Jesuit missionaries most likely wanted to honor the Apostles by naming a beautiful place after them, despite the actual number of islands.

Looking out over Lake Superior at the collection of forested islands, it's easy to imagine why the missionaries felt they'd discovered a place where the Spirit was present in a special way. Centuries before them, the Ojibwe Indians had also proclaimed the waters of the great lake as sacred. Even the rocks around Lake Superior were believed to be inhabited by tiny spirits. The visitor to the Apostle Islands will find beaches, sand dunes, sea caves, cliffs, remnant old-growth forests, and abundant wildlife.

Madeline Island, the largest of the islands, was inhabited by the Ojibwe for hundreds of years before the Europeans arrived in the 1660s; it remains the tribe's spiritual home. The Jesuits Claude Allouez and Jacques Marquette established a mission at **La Pointe du Saint Espirit** ("The Place of the Holy Spirit") on the island; the community is considered Wisconsin's oldest settlement. Today's visitors to La Pointe can visit the **La Pointe Indian Cemetery** (est. 1836, but dating back to 1793), a place of rest for Christianized Ojibwe, with miniature houses that protect food left for the dead as sustenance for their four-day journey to the hereafter. The Ojibwe Chief Great Buffalo is buried here; a defaced stone marks his grave. His son, Chief Little Buffalo, is buried amid four pines down the road where a marker and reflecting pond are dedicated to the Ojibwe chief and clansmen, called **Ojibwe Memorial Park**. Every Memorial Day the site is honored with drumming and a sacred fire.

La Pointe is also the former site of **Holy Family**, the first Catholic Church in Wisconsin, built by Father Frederic Bergna in 1835. Bergna led a mission there until 1843, holding services in English and Ojibwe. (The current building, in Bayfield, was built between 1898 and 1900 on what is known as "Catholic Hill.") Today, another Catholic church from the 1800s, **St. Joseph's**, still exists in the city of La Pointe, with a cemetery dating to the early 1800s. Nearby, the historic **St. John's United Church of Christ**, organized in 1921, overlooks Lake Superior. The present church building was completed in 1925. Its phone number is (715) 747-3903. Russian Revolution survivor Count Henselofsky created the painting of Christ that hangs over the altar. The current church has roots in the former **Mission House** (1833), which is now the post office and is identified with a plaque.

Madeline Island is accessible via ferry from Bayfield.
For ferry schedules and information, call (715) 747-2051.

The rugged shore of one of the Apostle Islands

A cruise service provides narrated tours around the National Lakeshore. One of the more noteworthy sites visible from the boat is Devil's Island, which rests atop many natural caves. Air pockets form under the island, causing a booming sound which natives attributed to angry spirits—hence the name. The island is also known as Manitou Island, named after the spirit said to reside there. Several other islands are named for natural features explained by legends.

Scheduled ranger-guided tours and walks are available seasonally. For those wishing to camp overnight, Apostle Islands National Lakeshore charges a camping permit fee.

Located on the south shore of Lake Superior, Ashland and Bayfield Counties.
The headquarters and visitors center is one block off Highway 13,
Bayfield, 23 miles north of Ashland and 90 miles east of Duluth,
Minnesota, (715) 779-3397. nps.gov/apis/

Ojibwe Reservation Sites

Lac Court Oreilles Reservation

Today the site of Honor the Earth Homecoming Powwow, the largest traditional powwow in North America, the Lac Court Oreilles Reservation was originally Sioux territory and then belonged to the Ottawa in the 1650s. Ojibwe since 1765, the land is sacred to the Lac Court Oreilles Band, who formed a reservation there in 1854.

Lac Court Oreilles is a French name meaning "short ears," because the Native Americans in the area did not elongate their earlobes as some of the other eastern tribes did.

The Homecoming Powwow began as a peaceful protest against the National State Power Company, which flooded the many of the ricing beds, grace sites, and homes on the land in 1923.

Located near Couderay, on Highway 70/27, Sawyer County. glitc.org/lco.htm

With a mission for healing both body and spirit, the **Abiinooji-Aki Cultural Healing Center** provides programs like the Anishinaabe Way, to "help individuals and families to overcome the destructiveness and devastation that results from living in a negative environment." Family issues of alcoholism and violence are among the topics discussed and combined with traditional teachings. Programs include "Youth at Risk," "Healing the Healing Professional," and "Celebration of Sobriety Powwow."

Located on tribal lands, Sawyer County, (715) 634-5806.

Lac du Flambeau Reservation

The "Lake of Flames" was named after the sight of Ojibwe fishing at night with their torches. The Indian Bowl was a permanent settlement for Ojibwe that dates back to 1745. The legendary Chief Kees-Ke-Mun, said to be leader of all Ojibwe (Chippewa) settlements from Lake Superior to the Fox River and from Sault Ste. Marie to the Mississippi, led the tribe.

Today, the area is the site of weekly powwows, every Tuesday from the last Tuesday in June through the third Tuesday in August. A special Fourth of July powwow and a rodeo in late August are also held. There is a small admission charge. Visitors are asked to "bring a seat cushion and insect repellent . . . [but] don't bring a watch, a business suit, a schedule, or a rain cloud." Visitors can tour the museum and gift shop by appointment from May 1 through October 31, take part in workshops teaching about Native American culture, and watch "living history presentations."

Powwows are held in the Indian Bowl, on Highway 47 at County D in downtown Lac du Flambeau, about 10 miles northwest of Woodruff, Vilas County. The museum and cultural center are just south of the Indian Bowl. Information is available by contacting the Lac du Flambeau Band of Lake Superior Chippewa at (715) 588-3333. Information on camping is available at (715) 588-9611. glitc.org/ldf.htm

A visit to the Indian Village at **Wa-Swa-Goning** is truly a visit back in time to when the Ojibwe lived off the land. Literally, the "Place Where They Spear Fish with Torches," located on the Lac du Flambeau Ojibwe reservation, features an authentic cedar lodge, smokehouse, canoe arbor, ricing pit, and Native American camps complete with tepees and wigwams.

The village is so authentic, it's been used in motion pictures and documentaries and has received the State of Wisconsin Historic Trust Preservation Award for reservation of history. It sits on 20 acres of forestland along Moving Cloud Lake.

Created by Nick Hockings as an educational facility, Wa-Swa-Goning exists to help people understand the ways of Native Americans. "Whatever people do not understand, they fear, and what they fear they try to destroy," says Hockings. The village offers a variety of activities for visitors, including scouts and school groups. Women's spiritual sessions, sweat lodges, and youth rites are among the special events. About 5,000 people visit the facility each year.

Tours are available from 10 a.m. to 4 p.m. Tuesday though Saturday, from mid-June through September. Group tours (15 or more) can be arranged by calling in advance. Admission is $7 for adults and $6 for children 5 to 12 and those over 65.

Located at County H and Highway 47, just east of Lac du Flambeau, Vilas County, (715) 588-2615. waswagoning.com; turtle-island.com/waswagoning.html; pages.prodigy.net/egr3/was1.html

A traditional tree bark lodge at Wa-Swa-Goning, Lac du Flambeau

Bad River Reservation

The largest of the six Ojibwe reservations in Wisconsin, Bad River Reservation is more than 123,000 acres, much of it along Lake Superior shoreline. The only settlement there is Odanah (the Ojibwe word for "town"), five miles east of Ashland on Highway 2. The "Living Center," a log heritage complex on Highway 2, serves as a location for traditional tribal funerals and also features a museum and educational arts and crafts.

More than 95 percent of the land on the reservation is undeveloped. Bad River Sloughs, an everglade-type area, is especially significant to Ojibwe who have sustained their lives by harvesting wild rice there.

The mythical "Little People" are said to live at Marble Point, at the eastern edge of the reservation on Lake Superior. The stones in the area are said to be unusually round, the product of the work of the fairy people. Native Americans avoid the area, except to get special charms for their Medewin ceremony. To kill game or cut a tree in the area invokes the wrath of the Little People. Gigito-Mikana, the old Native American trail, was the site of an Ojibwe celebrated council.

Located along Highway 2 in eastern Ashland County. For more information, call (715) 682-7111. glitc.org/badriv1.htm, glitc.org/badriv1.htm

Native American Mission Churches

St. Francis of Assisi, Flambeau Mission Church

The Flambeau Mission Church is on the National Register of Historic Places. The Roman Catholic Mission was the principle effort of Father Francis Goldsmith, who would travel once or twice a year to Flambeau for services from 1869 to 1879. The landmark church was built in 1881 and dedicated in 1883. The bell tower was added later. The small chapel now serves as a mission of St. Mary's Catholic Church in Bruce, Wisconsin. Services are conducted between Memorial Day and Labor Day.

Located off County D, along the Flambeau River, Rusk County. From Ladysmith, take Highway 27 south for about 15 miles to County D; turn west.

St. Francis Solanus Indian Mission

This church features a wigwam tabernacle and gift shop selling Native American arts and crafts such as quilts and beadwork. Established in 1880 and built in 1924, the church is open daily, but arrangements must be made to see the gift shop.

Located at County E on the Lac Courte de Oreilles Reservation, Sawyer County.

St Joseph's Roman Catholic Mission, La Pointe
(See Apostle Islands, earlier in this chapter.)

St. John's United Church of Christ, La Pointe
(See Apostle Islands, earlier in this chapter.)

Winnebago Indian Mission, UCC

"Enter to worship, depart to serve," says the sign at the former Winnebago Indian Mission, now a United Church of Christ congregation after its reorganization in 1922. Members of the German Reformed Church founded the original mission church in 1878. Jacob Hauser, who had been a missionary in India, was confirmed in his work by Chief Black Hawk, who said, "The words you have spoken are good. We also believe in Earthmaker. We love our children. It will make us glad to see them well taught. We are glad you have come." At its peak, the mission included about half the Ho-Chunk population of Jackson County, powwow grounds, and Native American cemetery. There is a Wisconsin official marker, "Winnebago Indians," at the westbound Interstate 94 rest area in Jackson County.

Located at W8870 Mission Drive, 7 miles
east of Black River Falls, Jackson County.

Parks, Mound Groups, and Other Related Sites

Council Grounds State Park

A traditional gathering location for the Ojibwe, the Council Grounds was used for annual tribal festivals. Tribe members traveled there by canoe on the nearby Wisconsin River each year for several days and nights of celebration.

Located 2 miles northwest of Merrill on Highway 64 at Highway 107,
Lincoln County. co.lincoln.wi.us/html/council_grounds.html

Winneboujou

According to Ojibwe legend, Winneboujou, "the giant blacksmith" Manitou created the first man here. He used a flat-topped granite peak for his anvil. The first man was a hero/demigod who slept on the banks of the Brule River. When a strong southerly wind blew him far out into the lake, he blew his whistle and the North Wind brought him back.

Winneboujou was credited with creating copper weapons, and hearing the sound of his hammer was considered a blessing by the Ojibwe and was greatly feared by the Sioux. Some report still hearing the sounds today. The Northern Lights have been attributed to the sparks from his forge fire. Manitou's summer home was at the source of the Brule River. The town of Winneboujou is in Bayfield County.

Lake Marinuka

This lake is named for Indian Princess Marie Nounka, daughter of Chief Winneshiek and granddaughter of Winnebago Chief One-Eyed Decorah. After her death in 1884 at the ripe old age of 82, she was given a traditional burial-buried at midnight at the head of the lake with her head facing north. But her grave has since been moved twice—once when a barn was built too close to it, and once when the site was needed by the fire department. Visitors can find her grave today at the northwest side of the lake on County T.

Located on County T near Highway 93/54,
Galesville, Trempealeau County.

Maiden Rock

There's an official Wisconsin historical marker on the bluff named for the legend of the anguished Native American girl who's said to have taken her own life there. Her name, her tribe, and the exact circumstances vary depending on who's telling the tale. The parts of the story that remain constant are these: a beautiful young Indian maiden had fallen in love, but not with the man she was expected to marry.

Her family, her tribe, and especially her father refused to listen to her pleadings to marry the man she loved, who was from another tribe. In some accounts, her beloved was sent away; in others, he was ordered to be killed. In one version of the story, the maiden jumps off the bluff in grief after watching her beloved die of an arrow wound. At the end of all the stories, though, the maiden's grieved father finds her crushed body at the foot of the bluff. The township, the town, and the bluff itself are all named after this tragic legendary figure.

Located on the Mississippi River off County S, Pierce County;
it's approximately 10 miles north of Pepin and across the river
from Red Wing, Minnesota. mississippi-river.org/maiden.html

Indian Mounds Campground

Part of the Northern Highlands and American Legion State Forests, these four conical mounds can be viewed from a picnic area adjacent to Lake Tomahawk.

Located on Highway 47, 2 miles north of the community
of Lake Tomahawk, Oneida County.

Powers Bluff Park

Three different tribes—Ojibwe, Potawatomi, and Ho-Chunk—occupied this, the highest point (1,472 feet) in Wood County. Within the park are two native dance rings and two cemeteries, making the park sacred land. The park offers a mile-and-a-half self-guided hike.

Located southeast of Marshfield, on County E south of County N,
between the towns of Bethel and Arpin, Wood County.
Wood County Parks: (715) 421-8422.

Wakanda Park Mounds

Beside this lake, which is a widening of the Red Cedar River, three large oval mounds overlook the water. Seventeen other mounds are thought to be flooded. The mounds are believed to be burial mounds, probably erected by the Dakotas or Sioux, and the park was a former Indian village site.

Located off Pine Street in upper Wakanda Park,
Menomonie, Dunn County.

Trempealeau Mounds

Listed on the National Register of Historic Places, these mounds are located on the east bank of the mouth of the Trempealeau River near Mount Trempealeau.

Located in Perot State Park on Highway 35, Trempealeau County.

Rice Lake Indian Mounds Group

Twelve unusual "tailed" conical mounds are preserved behind the fairgrounds here. They are part of a group of 67 mounds. Excavations have uncovered burial bundles, ornaments, and items believed to have belonged to the Dakota Sioux. The mounds date back to pre-Columbian times. All together, the county has about 250 burial mounds—more than any other region of the same size in this part of the state. The site (also known as Indian Mounds Group) is on the National Register of Historic Places.

Located at Indian Mounds Park on Lakeshore Drive,
Rice Lake, Barron County.

Indian Mounds Park, Rice Lake

Portage County Cairns

An ancient Indian calendar site in Portage County has been called Wisconsin's Rockhenge. Professor James Sherz determined with aerial photography that strange islands, higher patches above the bogs, were composed of man-made effigies and purposefully placed rocks and rock formations. The effigies include a fish, rabbit, and snake—not the usual effigy types. With an assistant, Sherz mapped the prominent rocks, islands, and rock cairns. He found that astronomical alignments exist, especially solstices and equinoxes. The fact that people took the time and energy to create these cairns and mounds indicates they attributed a certain sacred quality to the area. The mapped area is mostly inaccessible marshland at this time and not conducive to visitation.

Located near Wisconsin Rapids, Portage County.
science-frontiers.com/sf034/sf034p01.htm

Boulder Effigy Mound

Discovered in 1902, the gigantic "bow and arrow" boulder effigy was observed by archaeologist Jacob V. Brower in 1902, who wrote, "Some of the stones representing the bowstring are misplaced. The intention seems to have been to represent a bow and arrow drawn to shoot toward Lake Pepin." More recently the effigy has been described as a bird. Its age is unknown, but it is believed to be ancient. It's not part of Indian lore of the region. The boulder effigy is the only one known in Wisconsin.

Located along Highway 63, 1 mile south of Highway 35,
near Hager City, Pierce County.

Wisconsin River Headwaters

According to Winnebago legend, an immense serpent formed the bed of the Wisconsin River. While traveling from his home in the northern forests to the sea, his body wore a deep groove into the ground, into which the water flowed to form the 300-mile river. The river's headwaters are close to Lac Vieux Desert. One early name for the stream, *Wees-konsan,* was Algonquin for "the gathering of the waters." We call it Wisconsin today.

Lac Vieux Desert County Park land has always been a sacred place to the Native Americans. The beginnings of the great river are so small that one could imagine jumping across it. Across the lake is the Upper Peninsula of Michigan.

Located off Highway 45 on County E, south of Land o' Lakes and 10 miles
north of Eagle River, Vilas County. Vilas County Parks: (715) 479-5160.
watersmeet.org/lacvieux.html

Manitou Falls

Manitou Falls are named after the Ojibwe Great Spirit. The Big Manitou Falls are 165 feet high, making them the highest waterfalls in the state. Little Manitou is a beautiful falls at 31 feet. It is easy to see the sacredness in the presence of these waterfalls. The 1,370-acre park includes camping and a beach on Interfalls Lake.

Located at Pattison State Park on the Black River, Highway 35,
south of Superior, Douglas County, (715) 399-3111.

Copper Falls State Park

This extraordinary park is among the most beautiful in the state, featuring several waterfalls and a narrow gorge with 100-foot walls. Falls vary from 10 to 40 feet. Paths are wheelchair accessible, and there are hiking trails, picnic areas, and 55 campsites.

Located 2 miles north of Mellen on Highway 169, Ashland County, (715) 274-5123.
silentsports.net/features/copper_falls_state_park.html

Copper Falls State Park, Mellen

Old Man of the Dalles, Interstate Park

Look at a Wisconsin map with a little imagination, and you'll see why Indianhead country is so named—the northwest corner of the state is shaped like the head of a Native American chief. Amazingly, a natural rock formation created during the glacier period in the bluffs at St. Croix Falls bears the same likeness. The Ojibwe believed the face was the image of the god Winneboujou. Today, it's known as the Old Man of the Dalles and is probably the most visited attraction in Interstate Park. There are legends about the Ojibwe enemies, the Dakotas, who were killed in the waters below.

Other naturally formed figures in the area include the Devil's Chair, Devil's Kitchen, and the Cross.

It was here that in about 1770 the Ojibwe battled against the Sioux and Fox, enemies of both the Ojibwe and the white settlers. With the Ojibwe victory, white settlers were able to move in to the area.

Located on Highway 8, St. Croix Falls, Polk County, at the Minnesota border.
wildernessinquiry.org/mnparks/parks/interstate5.htm

The "Spirits" of Wisconsin

A town, river, and lake in the area are all named "Spirit," as are a waterfall and flowage. The river runs along Highway 86, just southeast of Timms Hill, at 1,952 feet—the highest point in Wisconsin. The falls and flowage are located at County T and Highway 86 near Tomahawk in Lincoln County. The town of Spirit is located on Highway 86 at Highway 102 in Price County.

Dove Effigy Peace Mound

Part of Highground, Wisconsin's 140-acre Vietnam Veterans Memorial Park, the Dove Effigy was created by David Giffey, a Madison artist who is also an Eastern Orthodox iconographer. The 100-by-140-foot mound pays tribute to those who are or were prisoners of war and those who are missing in action and includes soil from all 72 counties of Wisconsin and from throughout the United States. There is a duplicate mound in Vietnam also dedicated to peace.

Vietnam veteran John Beaudin called the site "a spiritual place where you can go and let your mother the Earth hold you. Let the children play on it. Dance on it. Use it to unload your grief and pain. To renew and strengthen you. Lie back in the soft fold of its wings and let Mother Earth unburden you. Then get up and leave your troubles and cares there on the mound as you walk away renewed and refreshed."

Other features of Highground include the Vietnam Veterans Memorial, the National Native American Vietnam Veterans Memorial, and the home of the annual Warrior Powwow. The site is open to the public at no charge 24 hours a day, 365 days a year.

Located 2.5 miles west of Neillsville on Highway 10, Clark County, (715) 743-4224. thehighground.org/dove.html

Eastern Orthodox Sites

Holy Trinity Orthodox Church

Carpatho-Russian immigrants founded the parish in 1902. The first building was dedicated to St. Michael. In 1915 the original log building burned to the ground, and a new brick building was completed in 1921. It was consecrated in 1930 as Holy Trinity. The building features an onion dome with a Russian (three-armed) cross. About 30 families from the rural towns of River Falls, Rice Lake, Richmond, and other communities are served there. Regular services are held. The church is under the Orthodox Church in America, a former Russian jurisdiction.

Located at 523 First Street (1 mile south of County D), southeast of Clayton, Barron County, (715) 948-2203.

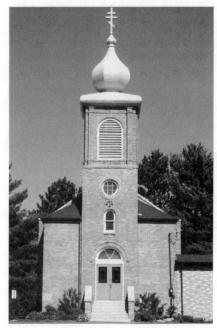

Holy Trinity Orthodox Church, near Clayton

St. Mary's Orthodox Church

Orthodox Christians of Slavic background established this church in 1906. Most had moved to northwest Wisconsin with the promise of employment in the logging industry and the promise of land ownership. The church, with an octagonal tower, green onion-shaped cupola, and Russian crosses, is set in the woods at the edge of the Lake Superior village of Cornucopia. The church is under the Orthodox Church in America, a former Russian jurisdiction.

Located in Cornucopia, northwest of Bayfield, Bayfield County. From Highway 13, turn east on County C; at the end of Eric Avenue (the third intersection), turn right.

Holy Assumption Orthodox Church

Established in 1908, Holy Assumption congregation built the current building in 1923. Its silver onion domes make it easily recognizable. There is a cemetery with a large prominent Russian-style cross as a memorial. The church is under the Orthodox Church in America, a former Russian jurisdiction.

Located at N1249 County F, Lublin, Taylor County, (715) 669-3855.

St. John the Baptist Orthodox Church

Established in 1906, it is the sister church to Holy Assumption (previous entry). This church is under the Orthodox Church in America, a former Russian jurisdiction. The diocese has not assigned a priest to this chapel. At this writing, services are held the fourth Sunday of the month.

Located north of Stanley, Chippewa County. Take County H north from Stanley about 10 miles to Shirley Road; turn left (west) to County G. The church is just past the tiny village of Huron on the left, (651) 631-0265.

Catholic Sites

Rudolph Grotto Gardens and Wonder Cave

A great place to bring children, Rudolph Grotto Gardens and Wonder Cave was created by Father Philip Wagner over the course of decades, starting in the 1920s and ending in the spring of 1983. For Father Wagner, creating the grotto was a promise he'd made to God after a miraculous healing. Today the grotto is considered a memorial to the faith and devotion of Father Wagner.

The complex series of grottoes, bridges, and walkways provides space for prayer and reflection. Religious art, symbolism, and Biblical scenes are found throughout. The "cave" is actually aboveground, but it gives the feeling of being underground. It is has 18 shrines depicting the life and teachings of Jesus Christ. In 1950, after being criticized by his bishop for spending years on the "nonsensical" series of caves, Wagner built a conventional church, St. Philip the Apostle.

Today one can choose to spend several hours at the grotto gardens. Its 40 attractions include Stations of the Cross, Stations of the Seven Sorrows of Mary, the Last Supper, a Lourdes Shrine, a museum, a Fatima Shrine, and a war memorial.

There is a small admission to the cave, but the rest of the attraction is free. It's open year-round during daylight hours. Meals are provided on a reservation basis for groups of 30 or more. A gift shop and the Wonder Cave are open Memorial Day to Labor Day, from 10 a.m. to 5 p.m.

Located at 6957 Grotto Avenue (at Highway 34 and County C), Rudolph, Wood County (15 miles west of Stevens Point). Information or meal reservations are available by calling (715) 435-3456 (evenings) or (715) 435-3120.

Cathedral of Christ the King

Louis Preuss designed this replica of the church of Santa Maria Maggiore in Rome. The cathedral has a basilica feel to its architecture with a long stairway to a beautiful portico and a Romanesque tower. It was dedicated in 1927.

Located at 1115 Belknap Street, Superior, Douglas County, (715) 392-8511.

Sacred Heart of Jesus Catholic Church

On Catholic Hill, a statue of Christ has arms stretched in blessings over the city of Eau Claire. The statue is next to Sacred Heart Church. This "imposing example of late neo-Romanesque architecture," as it says on a wall plate at the front of the church, was built in 1929 to replace the original building, built in 1875. St. Joseph Kapela Chapel, erected by Father Joseph Boehm, is part of Sacred Heart Cemetery, founded in 1882. The 1896 chapel is on the National Register of Historic Places. The chapel and cemetery are under the administration of Sacred Heart Parish.

Church is located at 418 N. Dewey Street, Eau Claire, Eau Claire County, (715) 830-2275. Cemetery and chapel are located on Omaha Street, Eau Claire. rc.net/lacrosse/stpat

On Catholic Hill, a statue of Christ above the city of Eau Claire

St. Ann's Catholic Church and Cemetery

Dating to 1888, St. Ann's is on the National Register of Historic Places. The church, built by Bohemian German settlers, stands on the hillside overlooking the cemetery where many founding members of the community now rest. Due to a shortage of priests, the church was closed in 1963. The building was restored in the 1980s as a historic site. The structure is considered to be Romanesque and the altar Byzantine Romanesque. Features include the three tower bells (Anna, Mary Theresa, and Elizabeth), purchased in 1892 for $197.67. The structure is one of the oldest church buildings remaining in the Diocese of Superior.

Located at W3963 Brehm Avenue, 5 miles southwest of Rib Lake, Taylor County.

St. Bede Retreat and Conference Center

St. Bede's was established in the late 1970s as a retreat and conference center. This Benedictine community of women provides staff-directed retreats for individuals and groups. The structure of the priory "blends medieval and modern motifs," and the simple chapel is intended to focus attention "on the altar of the Eucharist and the lectern of the Word."

The Center offers a variety of meeting rooms and can accommodate 150 people for a conference or overnight accommodations for 30.

Located at 1190 Priory Road, Eau Claire, Eau Claire County, (715) 834-8642.

St. Clare Center for Spirituality

Dating back to 1874, St. Clare Center is sponsored by the Felician Sisters, Third Order of St. Francis. An orphanage for boys operated there until 1936.

The Center's mission is to provide "a joyful, hospitable, and prayer-filled atmosphere where all may grow in relationship to their Creator and Redeemer." Examples of retreats offered include "Reflections for Lent," "Writing Your Journey," and a "Jesus Day" retreat for children. Group retreats follow themes and must be arranged at least a month in advance. Guided and directed retreats, as well as private retreats for individuals, are also available. A donation is requested.

Features of St. Clare include an extraordinarily beautiful chapel, saint's grottoes, and the **Sacred Heart of Mary Shrine**. The shrine dates back to 1910 and has since been expanded. Favors granted at the shrine are said to include successful surgery, court cases settled favorably, and the cure of a "blue baby" who later married and became the father of two children.

Located at 7381 Church Street, Polonia, near Custer, Portage County.
Information on enrollment is available by calling (715) 592-4099.

Sacred Heart of Mary Shrine at the St. Clare Center for Spirituality, Polonia

St. Anthony Retreat Center

Built in 1918, the Center was a seminary for Capuchin fathers until 1970. It is located on 55 acres of wooded land just outside of Marathon.

Located a quarter mile west of Marathon, Marathon County,
(715) 442-2236. sarcenter.com

ther Sites

Christ Episcopal Church

Built in 1870, Christ Church was the first Episcopal church in northern Wisconsin. The building, which is said to look like a gingerbread house, is listed on the National Register of Historic Places.

Located at 121–125 N. Third Street, Bayfield,
Bayfield County, (715) 779-3401.

Christ Church Cathedral

A good example of early 20th-century neo-Gothic Revival style, this Episcopal Church building was finished in 1916. Christ Church was named the Diocesan Cathedral of Eau Claire in 1931. The Chapel of the Ascension, used for daily services, was built four years later. A plaque at the door reads "Daily Services, Always Open."

A special feature is the Gloria Dei bell tower with 14 bells each named for a saint. Completed in spring of 1996, the structure was started in 1977. Each bronze bell is inscribed with a portion of the 121st Psalm, and when taken together, the bells weigh more than one and a half tons.

Located at 510 S. Farwell Street, Eau Claire,
Eau Claire County, (715) 835-3734.

Holy Island

This large peninsula at the southern tip of Long Lake provided the spot for a retreat center established by a group of Norwegian Lutheran ministers from different churches. The peninsula is now residential, but there remains a quiet bench at the end of the scenic drive where one can meditate in the middle of Long Lake.

Located on Holy Island Road, off County D (right turn after
County MD), at Long Lake, about 8 miles north of
Rice Lake, Washburn County.

Sabylund Lutheran Church

This red brick Swedish Lutheran church has an awesome approach through a cedar-lined driveway. The church is a parish of the Evangelical Lutheran Church of America. Its history dates back to 1856, when Swedish immigrants started settling this area of the state. The present church was built in 1893.

Located at W11137 County J, near Stockholm, Pepin County. At Stockholm,
turn on County J from Highway 35 and go northeast about 5 miles
(the church is a quarter mile south of Lund), (715) 448-4044.

Sabylund Lutheran Church, near Stockholm

Christ Guide Us

The subject of intense controversy between the city of Marshfield and the Freedom From Religion Foundation, this 15-foot statue of Jesus Christ standing on planet Earth greets travelers on Highway 13 as they enter the city.

The Knights of Columbus gave the statue to the city in 1959; in 1998, the city was sued on the basis that the statue should not be on public property. Later, the piece of land immediately surrounding the statue was sold to a private owner, and a three-foot wall was to be erected around the statue to separate the private property from the public property—but some argued the fence would only accentuate the statue. Since then, legal battles have continued. One thing is sure—the statue has received much more public attention due to the lawsuit than it would have without it.

*Located at the Praschak Wayside on Highway 13,
Marshfield, Wood County.*

Amish and Mennonite Communities

Wisconsin is home to several Amish communities. The Amish and Mennonite groups trace their origins to 16th-century Switzerland, when a group called the Anabaptists (rebaptizers) formed a fellowship. They believed that people should be baptized as adults rather than as infants, and they wanted a church that was not under the control of the state.

The Mennonites developed from one of the Anabaptist groups, named after a former Catholic priest, Menno Simons, who joined the group in 1536. The Amish resulted from a split from the Mennonites, when Jacob Amman broke from the fellowship over a disagreement about excommunication.

Mennonites taught pacifism and separated themselves from society; the Amish went a step further, with the Old Order Amish retaining dress and customs of the 18th century. Their wide-brimmed hats and horses and buggies are familiar sights in Taylor and Eau Claire Counties. The oldest continuous Amish community in Wisconsin is located in Medford, Taylor County.

Old Order Amish dress "plain," with dark suits, wide-brimmed hats, and long dresses. Modern inventions such as buttons are forbidden, and, of course, the Amish must use buggies rather than automobiles for transportation. Other Amish and Mennonites are allowed various levels of modernity in dress and lifestyle. Many Amish families take part in Saturday farmers' markets around the state, selling their crops.

The German Mennonite farming colony of Soloma was settled around 1900. The name was derived from a combination of Sharon (a Biblical reference to a place with abundant pastures), and the name of Frank Sauer, one of colony's founders.

When driving in Amish areas, one is asked to be respectful of the buggies and not to take photos of the people, as photography is considered a forbidden "graven image."

Tours of Amish areas in western Wisconsin start in Westby, Crawford County. Call (608) 654-5318 for information.

Marynook Retreat and Conference Center

Under the Society of Mary, this ecumenical conference center offers 40 sleeping rooms, a conference room and dining hall, chapel, library, and gift shop. The grounds were formerly those of Galesville University, the second university in the state of Wisconsin.

Located at 500 S. 12th Street, Galesville, Trempealeau County, about 20 miles north of La Crosse.

Moon Beach Camp, United Church of Christ

This ecumenical camp, conference, and retreat center is located between Eagle River and Saint Germaine. A variety of both generic and specialty camps are offered, including a single parent family camp, a "rainbow family" camp (for families with gay or lesbian heads of household), elderhostels, an Epiphany retreat during the Christmas season, and a "Jesus Core" camp for senior high youth and young adults. The camp is open year-round and has 20 cabins with heat and indoor plumbing.

Located at 7250 Birchwood Drive, off Highway 70, near St. Germaine, Vilas County, (715) 479-8255. ucci.org

The Woodlands

This beautiful facility calls itself a learning/demonstration center, a nature wonderment area, and a retreat/reflection space. Its mission "envisions a world where all people, the Earth, and her life community relate in ways that are mutually beneficial, fulfilling, and sustainable."

Located at N47475 Woodland Lane outside Osseo,
Trempealeau County, (715) 597-2711.

Christine Center

Formerly the Christine Center for Unitive Planetary Spirituality, the Christine Center is "dedicated to individual and spiritual transformation." The retreat center is located on 120 acres of central Wisconsin woodland and includes 13 hermitages and a new 8,500-square-foot facility.

Although started by Franciscan Sisters in 1980, the Center's mission and purpose has evolved, encouraging interreligious understanding and drawing from the unity of many spiritual traditions.

The Center's Web site says the Center is "dedicated to the recognition that all of Humanity is One Body. Underlying the diversity of cultural and socio-religious mythologies is a perennial tradition of mystical Unitive Spirituality. As Humanity comes to realize itself as One Body, the consciousness to respond to the environmental and social issues of the day will become apparent." Retreats, sabbaticals, meditation, workshops, spiritual guidance, bodywork, volunteer programs, and outdoor recreational activities are advertised.

Located at W8291 Mann Road, 3 miles south of Willard,
Clark County; turn left from County G (Mann Road is dirt),
(715) 267-7507. christinecenter.org

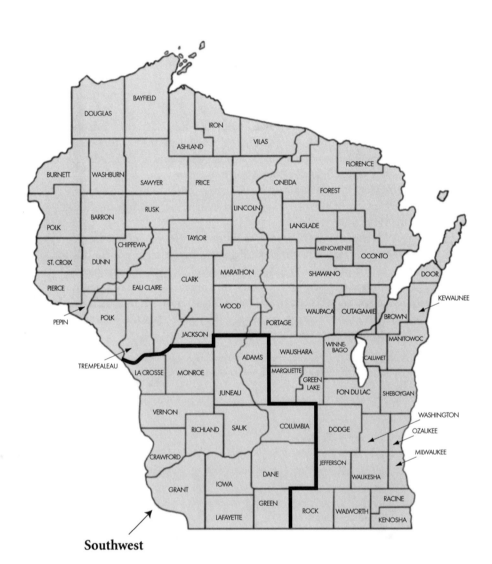

Southwest

Southwest Wisconsin

Including the counties of Adams, Columbia, Crawford, Dane, Grant, Green, Iowa, Juneau, La Crosse, Lafayette, Monroe, Richland, Sauk, and Vernon

Chapter 5

Southwest Wisconsin

W

e are inspired to look up even beyond to the heavens above.
This is a sacred place."

—inscription on a plaque at Durward's Glen

THERE ARE WHOLE counties in this region that do not have a straight stretch of highway for more than a mile or so off the Interstate system. This includes the Driftless Region, an area untouched by the glacial modifications that took place in northern and eastern Wisconsin. Perhaps this is one reason so many cultures have found this part of the state full of spiritual beings and the awesome wonders of creation. Certainly the effigy mound builders favored this region—particularly the area of what is now Dane County, where there are easily more effigy mounds than in any other place in the world.

Buddhists from Tibet and Cambodia have found homes in southern Wisconsin. His Holiness, the XIV Dalai Lama, has visited Madison at least five times, dedicating a Buddhist stupa (shrine) at Deer Park Buddhist Center in the Madison suburb of Oregon.

The lead mines at the southwestern corner of the state brought Christian diversity, Catholics and Lutherans in particular. There are beautiful examples of Lutheran churches, and most of the Catholic shrines and grottoes in the state are here (the grotto at Dickeyville is probably one of the most famous). The striking Chapel of Perpetual Adoration in La Crosse has seen uninterrupted prayer for more than 125 years.

This area is steeped in mysterious and unusual places, like the Wisconsin Dells, which despite its more commercial modern existence still awakens a sense of awe. Just south of the Dells is Devil's Lake (which has always been called Spirit Lake by Native Americans; the lake may be the victim of an unfortunate translation). Devil's Lake is known for the depths of the spring-fed lake and the heights of the bluffs and rock formations that surround it. The Wisconsin River and Mississippi River bluffs are places of wonder as well.

This is where a town called Little Norway claims a small valley called the Place of Elves and where there is a Troll Way through the Main Street of Mount Horeb. It should come as no surprise that this would be the place for the first federally recognized Wiccan church and nature sanctuary. Pagans gather for nature worship at Circle Sanctuary, which found its home near Barneveld in Iowa County.

Iowa County is also the home of legendary architect Frank Lloyd Wright. Taliesin, his estate, is snuggled in the Wisconsin River hills of his childhood. His family chapel, Unity Chapel, still bears his gravestone (but not his body) and those of his family. In Madison, First Unitarian Meeting House is one of the few churches he designed.

When planning the book, we almost included the Wisconsin State Capitol building, which is based on the ancient plans for a solar temple and is intentionally lined up with the four directions. It is filled with moral, ethical, and spiritual murals and art. But it seemed that inclusion might create confusion as to the current use of the building and the intent of this guide.

Favorite Sites

_◯ **Cathedral of St. Joseph the Workman, La Crosse**
   (modern Cathedral seating more than 1,000)

_◯ **Circle Sanctuary, Barneveld**
   (beautiful view from Spirit Rock, ideal for meditation)

_◯ **Dickeyville Grotto, Dickeyville** (world renowned and unique)

_◯ **Durward's Glen, Baraboo** (a beautiful retreat)

_◯ **Effigy Mound National Monument, Marquette, Iowa**
   (collection of effigy mounds with informative museum)

_◯ **Gates of Heaven Synagogue, Madison** (oldest synagogue in the Midwest)

꧁ **Kickapoo Indian Caverns, Wauzeka** (an exciting underground world)

꧁ **Koshkonong Prairie Lutheran Churches, Dane County**
(interesting history and architecture)

꧁ **Mahe-pinah Springs, Middleton** ("sacred springs" at former Ho-Chunk village)

꧁ **Man Mound Park, Baraboo** (unique man-shaped mound)

꧁ **Maria Angelorum Chapel, La Crosse**
(site of uninterrupted prayer since 1878)

꧁ **Mendota State Hospital Mound Group, Madison**
(the largest known and preserved eagle effigy in the world)

꧁ **Nelson Dewey Mound Group, Cassville**
(outstanding view overlooking Mississippi River)

꧁ **Pleasant Ridge Cemetery, Beetown** (former slaves settled here)

꧁ **Roche-A-Cri Petroglyphs, Friendship** (5,000-year-old rock carvings)

꧁ **Sinsinawa Mound Convent and Retreat Center, Sinsinawa**
(relics of saints, modern art, and a permanent outdoor labyrinth)

꧁ **Spirit Spring, Madison**
(the first spot in the area to turn green each spring)

꧁ **Plain Shrine at St. Anne's Hill, Plain** (well worth the tough climb)

꧁ **St. Augustine's Church, New Diggings** (oldest of the Mazzuchelli churches)

꧁ **St. Mary of the Oaks Chapel, Dane County**
(Germanic-style chapel built in thanks)

꧁ **St. Patrick's Catholic Church, Benton**
(Father Mazzuchelli's final resting place)

꧁ **Swiss United Church of Christ, New Glarus** (built by Swiss immigrants)

꧁ **Three Chimneys, Viroqua**
(thunder spirits are said to live atop the stone formations)

Spirit Spring, Madison

*M*ound Groups
Goodland County Park Mounds
(Baum Mound Group)

This is a set of three linear mounds and a conical mound in a group that covers the picnic area near the more-than-200-foot-long beach. As with most mound groups, these are on the National Register of Historic Places. These look almost like ripples in the land and are not clearly marked but are on both sides of Main Park Road.

Located on the west side of Lake Waubesa, just southeast of Madison.

Take Highway 14 to County MM to Goodland Park Road.

Indian Mound Park (Lewis Mound Group)

Two conical mounds, one oval mound, two linear mounds, a bear effigy, and an unusual hook-shaped mound (which was probably the tail of a serpent or panther mound) are featured in this high hill overlooking Lake Waubesa and Mud Lake. The hill is also home to the McFarland Water Tower. For the easiest access, park at the American Legion Post building on Burma Road and use the footpath. The mounds are in good condition and are on the National Register of Historic Places.

Located at McFarland City Park, Burma Road, McFarland, Dane County.

Blackhawk Country Club Mound Group

This site, on the National Register of Historic Places, includes an excellent example of a goose mound as well as linear mounds and a bear mound. The goose has a wingspread of 135 feet. The bear is 80 by 20 feet and is one of what used to be a grouping of three bears. A panther mound 119 feet long may have been meant to "guard" the other mounds. The grouping is also known as Wah Zhe Dha. These mounds have been incorporated into the club's golf course. Access is limited, so call the country club before visiting.

Located in Shorewood Hills along Lake Mendota Drive, Dane County.

Blackhawk Country Club, (608) 231-2454.

madisonmagazine.com/yourmadison/stories/yourmadison-features-20010107-133644.html

Burrows Park Bird Effigy Mound

In a small Madison park on Lake Mendota is this late woodland bird effigy mound with a wingspan of 128 feet. The mound was damaged but restored in 1934. It is on the National Register of Historic Places.

Located just east of the Burrows Park parking lot on Burrows Road, off Sherman Avenue, Madison, Dane County. wisconsinstories.org/2001season/native/nj_journey.html

Mendota State Hospital Mound Group

Two mound groups located on the grounds of what is now called the Mendota Mental Health Institute are among the largest and best-defined effigies in the world. On this point of land 70 feet above lake level are 11 conical mounds of various sizes, as well as linears, a bird, and a panther. Some other mounds were destroyed by the construction of the institute's buildings.

Eagle Mound on the grounds of the Mendota Mental Health Institute, Madison

Eagle Mound, behind the children's facility, may be the largest eagle effigy in the world, with an original wingspan of more than 624 feet. There are two other large eagle mounds on the grounds. Near the eagles are two panthers, a deer (unusual in that it has four legs), two bear mounds, and some conicals. These mounds face Lake Mendota and what is now downtown Madison. It is believed a stockaded Indian village was once in the area. The mounds are on the National Register of Historic Places.

Farwell's Point Mound Group is on a peninsula that is commonly called Governor's Island. The access road to the park is on the Mendota Institute grounds. The park has a pleasant nature trail and a large bear effigy along the way.

Located on the Mendota Mental Health Institute grounds, 1310 Troy Drive, Madison (near Westport), Dane County. For a guide and more information, it is requested that people stop in at the administration building. dhfs.state.wi.us/MH_Mendota/Mendota/mounds.htm

Morris Mound Group, Governor Nelson State Park

There is a 358-foot panther effigy mound and other mounds along the trails in the southern section of the 422-acre state park. The site was also an 18th-century Ho-Chunk village. The mounds can best be seen from the Woodland Trail or Morning Side Trail. On the northern shore of Lake Mendota are six conicals and a large panther mound. A guide showing the location of the mounds is available at the park office.

*Located at Governor Nelson State Park, on County M,
near Middleton and Waunakee, Dane County, (608) 831-3005.*

Observatory Hill Mounds

This site, next to the University of Wisconsin's observatory with one of the most scenic views of Lake Mendota, features a double-tailed turtle effigy mound, represented crawling over the ridge with the tails pointing toward the lake. Unfortunately the tails have worn away and are difficult to discern. There is also a bird effigy, which had an original wingspan of 133 feet. The plaque says the effigy is 500 years old, but today it's known to be much older—at least 1,000 years. Other mounds in the area have been destroyed.

*Located on Observatory Drive on the
UW-Madison Campus, Madison, Dane County.*

Pheasant Branch Hill Group

Situated on a hill with a view of the Pheasant Branch flowage to Lake Mendota, this hill has five mounds—four conical and a linear. There's some evidence that the site originally served an astronomical function. Friends of Pheasant Branch are working to preserve them for viewing. Currently the mounds reside under the brush and brambles at the top of the hill.

*Located in the Pheasant Hill Dane County Natural Area,
Pheasant Branch Road,
just north of Middleton, Dane County.*

Picnic Point Mound Group

Along the east shore of Picnic Point and along the south pedestrian path behind the UW Natatorium on Willow Drive are several conical mounds and a linear mound. Farming damaged the goose mound in the same vicinity. All the mounds are within yards of the Lake Mendota shore.

Located along Willow Drive on the UW-Madison Campus, Madison, Dane County.

Spring Harbor Mound Group, Madison

Spring Harbor Mound Group

Only one mound remains of those on this ridge overlooking the floodplain of Old Merrill Creek, north of the current Spring Harbor School. They were once part of a mound group of 50 that was one of four groups in this area. Also on the National Register of Historic Places, the well-preserved bear mound looks onto the school playground and parking lot. From that hillside, and before housing construction, one could easily see Lake Mendota. There are related mounds on private property in the area.

Located at Spring Harbor Drive, Madison, Dane County.

Edna Taylor Conservancy Mounds

This site features six linear mounds, one of which was originally more than 700 feet long, and a panther effigy mound on a high slope. The linear mounds are somewhat shortened due to farming and highway construction.

Located at Edna Taylor Conservancy, Femrite Drive, Madison, Dane County.

Elmside Park Mounds

Overlooking Lake Monona are two well-preserved effigies, believed to be a lynx and a bear. The mounds were part of a dense cluster that once existed between what is now Olbrich Park and the Yahara River. The site is on the National Register of Historic Places, and a plaque by the Madison Landmarks Commission dates the mounds at 500 to 1000 C.E. Nearby there is a sculpture in a storm-damaged tree, *Let the Great Spirits Soar*, carved by Harry Whitehorse, a Winnebago.

Located at Elmside Park, at the intersection of Lakeland and Maple Avenues, Madison, Dane County.

Hudson Park Effigy Mound

Hudson and Elmside parks were created to preserve effigy mounds in the area, part of a grouping of mounds between the Yahara River and Olbrich Park. One bird effigy with a wingspan of 568 feet was destroyed. Today a long-tailed water spirit mound is preserved there. The long-tailed effigy is a turtle, a lizard or a panther, overlooking Lake Monona.

Located at Hudson Park, at the intersection of Lakeland and Hudson Avenues, Madison, Dane County.

Outlet Mound

The Outlet Mound was one of 19 conical, oval mounds overlooking the outlet of Lake Monona. The mound, believed to be a burial mound, could be 2,000 years old. Most of the other mounds in the area have been destroyed. Saved from destruction by local residents and the Wisconsin Archaeological Society in 1944, the mound site was then donated to the city of Monona. The mound is vaguely reminiscent of the temple mounds at Aztalan, although Outlet Mound is a great deal smaller.

Located at Midwood and Ridgewood Avenues, Monona, Dane County.

Edgewood College Mound Group

A dozen mounds exist at this site, but most are now flattened and hard to discern. A large bird mound is near Woodrow Street close to Dee Ricci Hall and the college library; a historical marker denotes the site. Two conical mounds are located near the playground. Others are visible along Edgewood Drive. The mounds are on the National Register of Historic Places.

Located at Woodrow Street, off Monroe Avenue,
on the Edgewood College campus,
Madison, Dane County. edgewood.edu

Forest Hill Cemetery Mound Group

In this cemetery, established in 1858 and where many prominent Madisonians, including eight governors, are buried, are a goose effigy, two panther mounds, and a linear mound. The large bird effigy's head was destroyed when the railroad corridor was built behind the cemetery. The site is on the National Register of Historic Places. A map is available during cemetery office hours.

Located at 1 Speedway Road (at Regent Street),
Madison, Dane County, (608) 266-4720.

Gallistel Woods Mound Group

On the National Register of Historic Places, this site has two large effigy mounds. A map of all arboretum mounds is available at the McKay Center located in the middle of the arboretum. Other mounds at the 1,260-acre arboretum include bird and panther effigies, linear mounds, and conical mounds. A network of springs runs through Gallistel Woods into Lake Wingra. These have been named the Charles E. Brown Mounds in honor of the early advocate and cartographer of mounds throughout Wisconsin.

Located in the UW Arboretum,
on either side of McCaffrey Road, Madison,
Dane County, (608) 263-7888.

Vilas Circle Bear Effigy

Neighborhood developers created this small oval park (now a city of Madison park) in the 1890s to preserve a bear mound. The area also once contained linear and conical mounds. The effigy mound is on the National Register of Historic Places.

Located in the 1400 and 1500 blocks of Vilas Avenue,
near Lake Wingra, Madison, Dane County.

Vilas Park Effigy Mounds

Overlooking the Henry Vilas Park Zoo and Lake Wingra are six conical mounds, a bird mound, and a panther mound. When a plaque was dedicated in 1915, representatives of a dozen Native American tribes were at the ceremony. Part of another mound is near the otter cage inside the zoo, which has free admission.

Located at Wingra and Erin Streets,
near Lake Wingra, Madison, Dane County.

Devil's Lake Bird Effigy Mound
and Devil's Lake Mound Group

The Devil's Lake Bird Effigy Mound is most unusual—150 feet long with a forked tail and wings that bend downward at their pointed tips. Other mounds around the lake include bears, conicals, and linears. The bear was restored in 1922, the panther and linears in 1977. Many mounds in the area were destroyed by railroad construction. A brochure is available with a self-guided tour.

Archaeologists believe there were as many as 1,500 mounds in the Devil's Lake area that is now Sauk County. Of the 100 or so that remain, only a few dozen are in good shape. (See Devil's Lake, later in the chapter.)

Located at S5975 Devil's Lake Park Road
3 miles southeast of Baraboo, off Highway 12 and Highway 33,
Sauk County, (608) 356-8301.

Man Mound Park

One of only nine human effigy mounds ever recorded, the Man Mound has horns, as if the figure is wearing a horned headdress, suggesting he may have been modeled after a shaman. The man was originally 214 feet long and 30 feet across at the shoulders. He's been cut off at the knees because of the road built in 1905. He is oriented as if he is walking from the east. A wooden lookout platform provides an excellent view of his shape. Known throughout the world, the Man Mound is on the National Register of Historic Places. The park is part of the Sauk County park system, purchased by the county in 1907.

Located on Man Mound Road, about 8 miles northeast of Baraboo, Sauk County;
from Baraboo, take Highway 33 east to County T, turn north
and go 2 miles to Man Mound Road, then go 4 miles east.
Sauk County Parks, (608) 546-5011.

Terminal Moraine Mound Group

Two clusters of 111 mounds once ran along the Baraboo River, but now only a plaque commemorates what was once considered one of the largest mound groups in North America. The plaque, entitled "Indian Mounds and Village," is on Water Street east of the Circus Museum in Baraboo. It is placed at the site of Chief Car-a-maue-nee's village. His council house was in the midst of 7 effigy mounds, part of the 90 that comprised an unbroken series of mound groups through residential Baraboo. Twenty more were located on the county fairgrounds. These mounds included effigies of men, birds, and animals, as well as many conical mounds.

Located on Water Street, Baraboo, Sauk County.

Gee's Slough Mounds, New Lisbon

Gee's Slough Mound Group, Indian Mounds Park

A number of very well-preserved conical mounds and chained or linked mounds from the pre-Columbian era, as well as some linears and a panther mound, are located at this site on the Lemonweir River, which includes an informational plaque. Closed during the winter.

Located off Highway 12/16 southeast of New Lisbon on Indian Mound Road, Juneau County.

Cranberry Creek Mound Group

More than 180 mounds of various shapes that are among the best preserved anywhere are featured in this DNR State Natural Area near Necedah. It contains clusters of conical and effigy mounds attributed to the Woodland Period.

The northern cluster of mounds has suffered from plowing over the years. The southern cluster is unharmed. The mound group has been mapped since 1917. The land north of the area also contains many mounds but belongs to a private archaeological group and the Wisconsin River Power Company. The mounds are in woods and within wild forests.

Located about 10 miles north of Necedah, Juneau County;
take County G about 10 miles north to 8th Street,
then go west to the southeast corner of the State Natural Area.
dnr.state.wi.us/org/land/er/snas/snas203.htm

Kingsley Bend Indian Mounds

Originally a grouping of at least 22 mounds, this site features very well-preserved conical and bear mounds. The site is on the National Register of Historic Places and includes an official Wisconsin marker. Famed Wisconsin Dells photographer H. H. Bennett photographed the mounds. For those driving into the wayside, a long-tailed panther or water spirit mound is visible on the right. The other mounds are up the hill where trails lead around the large mounds. There is an eagle mound, among others, across the highway on private land with no clear access.

Located on Highway 16, near Wisconsin Dells, 1.5 miles southeast of
Highway 16/127, Columbia County. co.columbia.wi.us/about/history/mounds.asp

Ghost Eagles

Aerial photography shows the flattened former mounds on this farmland. One former mound is in the form of an eagle with a 1,300-foot wingspan, the largest bird mound ever recorded. The Ho-Chunk have proposed reconstruction of the effigy mound. This site is part of the proposed Ho-Chunk Cultural Park.

Located north of the Wisconsin River near Lone Rock and Muscoda, Sauk County.

Avoca Mound Group

The site also includes compound mounds, five linear mounds, and six conical mounds. Some of the mounds have white cement markers on top. There are also informational signs at the park corner by the mounds with concrete markers.

Located at Lakeside Park, East Lake Shore Drive
at North Eighth Street, Avoca, Iowa County.

Bird Effigy Mound

Once known as Eagle Effigy Mounds, this site now has only one remaining mound. This impressive eagle effigy, whose body is 52.5 feet with a wingspan of 133 feet, can be seen from the highway; the grass is groomed for better viewing.

Located on Highway 60 between Eagle Corners and Orion, west of Highway 80 and north of Muscoda and the Wisconsin River, Richland County.

Alfred Reed Mound Group, Wayside Mounds

This simple wayside features six conical mounds and three linear mounds, very well preserved and marked. The wayside is on the edge of the Lower Wisconsin River State Wildlife Area.

Located on Highway 60, west of Wauzeka and just west of Gran Grae Creek, town of Bridgeport, Crawford County.

Wyalusing State Park Mound Group

This outstanding park, 500 feet above the confluence of the Wisconsin and Mississippi Rivers, contains some of Wisconsin's most spectacular mound groups—bear, deer, turtle, conical, linear, and several compound mounds in good shape stretching along the bluff lines.

The park once contained more than 130 mounds in 21 groupings. The State Park Office has trail maps that indicate the mounds. Today 69 mounds are preserved in several groupings, including these:

—◦ Council Ground Mound Group, also called the Ball Field Mound Group (two bear effigy mounds)

—◦ Homestead Mound Group (effigies, linears and compound)

—◦ Rollway Point Mound Group (three linear and three conical along the top of the ridge)

—◦ Sentinel Ridge Mound Group, also called "Procession of the Mounds" (conicals, linears, compounds, and effigies for more than 200 feet along the bluff)

Located at Wyalusing State Park on County C, south of Prairie du Chien, Grant County. wyalusing.org/park/overview.htm; wyalusing.org/park/history.htm

Myrick Park Effigy Mound

This 25-foot in diameter conical mound and an effigy (turtle) mound are what remain of an original group of five. When one mound was excavated in the 1880s, fragments of pottery and bone were found. Also known as the Midway Mound Group, the site is attributed to the Turtle Clan. Chain fences and markers protect the mounds and identify them for all park visitors.

Located at Myrick Park, 2000 La Crosse Street, near the south edge of the La Crosse River Marsh, La Crosse, La Crosse County.

Nelson Dewey Mound Group

At this magnificent overlook to the Mississippi River are a large number of compound (connected) conical mounds. The site features more than 25 conical mounds, linears, and compound mounds that stretch out in a line along the bluffs. At the lookout point is a Centennial Tree, planted on Arbor Day 2000 to celebrate the 100th year of Wisconsin State Parks. The mound group is on the National Register of Historic Places.

Located at Nelson Dewey State Park, 2 miles north of Cassville on Highway VV, Grant County.

Effigy Mound National Monument

Across the Mississippi River from Prairie du Chien on the Iowa side is a great bear effigy mound 137 feet long. Effigy Mound National Monument is known for the line of "marching bear" effigy groupings. Although it's just barely outside of the state of Wisconsin, the Effigy Mound National Monument in Marquette, Iowa, is worth visiting for its historical museum and well-interpreted mound sites. The area features 191 known mounds, mostly linear and conical. The bear mounds are among 29 excellent examples of effigy mounds. The visitor center, including the museum, is open from 8 a.m. to 5 p.m. daily.

Located on Highway 76, 3 miles north of Marquette, Iowa. nps.gov/efmo

Other Native American Sites

Devil's Lake

With a name that is actually a mistranslation of the Ho-Chunk *Ta-wa-cun-chuk-dah* (meaning "Sacred Lake," "Holy Lake," or "Spirit Lake"), the name of Devil's Lake has never frightened people away. It remains one of the premier parks in the nation, "The Grand Canyon of the Midwest." This lake, surrounded by 500-foot cliffs, features some of the most beautiful scenery to be found anywhere and has been a gathering spot for people from a variety of religious traditions.

Devil's Needle rock formation at Devil's Lake State Park, Baraboo

Native Americans have lived in the area for 500 generations, leaving a number of mounds representing both the upper world and the lower world. One bird mound on the south side of the lake has a wingspan of 115 feet. There are also a panther mound and linear mounds. According to Ho-Chunk mythology, the lake was the birthplace of the Buffalo Clan. A buffalo was said to have climbed out of the water and then turned into a man. It was also the site of a legendary battle between the water spirits and thunderbirds, which created the bluffs. According to another tribal myth, the cliffs around the lake were formed when a meteor struck the lake, throwing up rock on all sides.

In more recent times, many religious groups have held church services at or near Devil's lake, including Baptists who held immersion services there.

Devil's Lake Park has 9,300 acres and 406 campsites; it's open all year long.

Located at S5975 Devil's Lake Park Road, 3 miles southeast of Baraboo, off Highway 12 and Highway 33, Sauk County, (608) 356-8301. devilslakewisconsin.com

Do-gee-rah Spring

Doo-gee-rah is one of the springs, according to an Indian belief, through which the spirit of animals entered the spirit world. This is one of many springs that feed Lake Wingra. The Spring Trail stonework design is attributed to Frank Lloyd Wright.

Located at the duck pond in the UW Arboretum, in the 3700 block of Nakoma Road, Madison, Dane County, (608) 263-7888.

Merrill Springs

"Wishing Spring" (dubbed by Dorothy Brown in 1948) is said to have the power to grant wishes. Native Americans visited it for blessings. Anyone can drink from it and make a wish. Merrill Springs are nearby in a small lakeshore park in a circular stone wall. The springs are known as *Matt-e-lo'-hanah'* in native Ho-Chunk language.

Located on Lake Mendota Drive near Spring Harbor Drive, Madison, Dane County.

Mahe-pinah Springs

These springs are at a historic hill encampment of Chief Black Hawk and, more important, were home to a Ho-Chunk village for many years. The central springs were called *Mahe-pinah* or "sacred springs." The French, passing through this area, called them Belle Fontaine or "beautiful springs." The springs are under the watch of the DNR and the Friends of Pheasant Branch because they are the principle feeder to the Pheasant Branch Creek, its flowage and wet-lands, as well Lake Mendota. On the hill there are several remaining mounds.

Located in the Pheasant Hill Dane County Natural Area,
Pheasant Branch Road, just north of Middleton, Dane County.

Spirit Spring (Big Spring)

Along the south shore of Lake Wingra are three springs only a short distance apart. The Spirit Spring (named "Big Spring" by arboretum officials) is said to have medicinal value and was never used for ordinary purposes. It is also claimed to be the first place in the region to turn green after winter has passed. There is a bench and lookout at this serene and popular spot. This is one of many springs that feed Lake Wingra.

Located in the Gallistel Woods, UW Arboretum,
on McCaffrey Road, Madison, Dane County, (608) 263-7888.

Token Creek Springs

Token Creek is named for the Native American practice of dropping a token of tobacco or another small gift into the creek when they crossed, to appease the spirits who lived there. Recently uncovered, the springs were hidden beneath a mill and dam. The springs have a water flow three times greater than any other springs in Dane County. There is an elevated boardwalk through the wetlands of this county park.

Located in Token Creek County Park, just off Highway 51
north of Madison and west of Sun Prairie, Dane County.

Sho-he-taka (Eagle Heights Woods)

Here, at the highest elevation on the south shore of Lake Mendota, the Ho-Chunk went to "horse hill" to fast and gain inspiration from the horse spirit that lived there. The woods include a very steep path to the top of the hill. From late fall to early spring, while the trees are without leaves, there is a wondrous lookout onto Lake Mendota.

Located next to the UW Eagle Heights student housing complex
on Lake Mendota Drive, Shorewood Hills, Dane County.

Monument Rock

This pillar of rock 60 feet high on the hillside may have served as a native sundial. It was considered sacred and used as a signpost.

Located 7 miles south of Viroqua, Vernon County.

Three Chimneys rock formation, Viroqua

Three Chimneys

Native Americans thought it sacrilegious to camp near these three sedimentary rock formations that jut out from the ground. Gods were believed to live on top of the "chimneys."

Located on Three Chimney Road off Highway 14/27/61,
midway between Viroqua and Westby, Vernon County.

Stones With Stories

Southwestern Wisconsin, especially from Adams and Juneau Counties south and west to the Mississippi River, has many sacred rock-art sites. Most are carved into sandstone; others are charcoal cave paintings. All are stringently protected due to their fragile nature. Under new law, it is a felony to cause any damage to rock art. A recent discovery of rock art was found near La Crosse by an amateur archeologist, but its discovery was not announced until a $5,000 steel barricade had secured the cave; even so, the exact location is not being released to the public.

Roche-A-Cri, the "rock of tears" or "crying rock" or "crevice in the rock" (from the French *roche-a-cris*), features 5,000-year-old petroglyphs of thunderbirds and mythical scenes that are still visible even though they continue to be weathered. Discovered in 1851 by surveyors, they have been a Wisconsin treasure and a source of speculation ever since. The mesa (rock formation) above the stone etchings looks like a medieval monastery. About 300 feet above the surrounding woods, it was once a rocky island in the glacial lake that once covered Wisconsin. The site is on the National Register of Historic Places.

Roche-A-Cri State Park is located on Highway 13, just north of Friendship, in Adams County. dnr.state.wi.us/org/land/parks/specific/roche-a-cri/specialevents.htm; dnr.state.wi.us/org/land/er/snas/snas183.htm

The **Lemonweir Glyphs** are probably related to Roche-A-Cri's thunderbirds. They feature a dragon or panther face in the rock that can be seen only from the Lemonweir River (Juneau County). The Lemonweir River was called *Cana-man-woi-sipe*, which means "child." The glyphs, along with those of Roche-A-Cri, seem to have the same pattern of mythology as the effigy mounds throughout the region.

Gottschall Rock Shelter Cave (Grant County) has perhaps the most famous petroglyphs in Wisconsin. The cave provided shelter for early native people. Rock paintings inside may be related to Aztalan. A unique sandstone-sculpted head, "red horn," was discovered and dated to 1000 C.E. According to legends, red horn was defeated by giants and decapitated, but his head was miraculously reattached and healed. Professor James Scherz of UW-Madison says that the unusual acoustics of the cave were held sacred by the ancient people of the area. Professor Robert Salzer of Beloit College gives tours of the cave, located in Grant County, every Sunday during the summer, starting at noon. The tours last until about 2:30 p.m. and include an opportunity to view the fascinating artifacts that excavations have uncovered. The tour gathers at the gazebo in the town of Avoca, across from the post office. Contact Professor Salzer through the Logan Museum of Anthropology at Beloit College, (608) 363-2119, to verify tours. nps.gov/efmo

Stand Rock Ceremonial Grounds

These are ancient ceremonial grounds for Ho-Chunk people. An amphitheater was built in the 1920s in the natural rock formations nestled in the bluffs of the Wisconsin River near the Wisconsin Dells. Run for many years by a nontribal business, the Ho-Chunk bought out the business (including the DNR lease) in 1998. There were nightly ceremonial demonstrations in the summertime, but these have been discontinued. The Ho-Chunk have plans to start them up again.

Located on County N, 3 miles north of Wisconsin Dells, Juneau County.

Blue Mound State Park

The blue haze that surrounds the hill on a clear day would indicate that Manitou, the Great Spirit who lived there, was smoking a sacred pipe. This is the highest point in southern Wisconsin. Native Americans were known to make arrows and scraping tools from the flint found at the hill.

Located on County F, off Highway 18/151, between Mt. Horeb and Barneveld, far eastern Iowa County.

Kickapoo Indian Caverns

Kickapoo Indian Caverns is Wisconsin's largest natural cavern system, even larger than the well-known Cave of the Mounds. Carved by an underground river that was part of a 400-million-year-old seabed, the cave provided shelter for hunting Native Americans for centuries.

Weddings have been held in the gigantic "Cathedral Room," which features a large hanging wooden cross. A gift shop, a Native American museum, and 40-minute tours are available. The cave now has well-lit cement walks and is open in the spring and summer, with group rates for 20 or more.

Located at W200 Rheinhollow Road, off Highway 60, west of Wauzeka, Crawford County, (608) 875-7723.

Lutheran Sites

Hauge Log Church

This 1852 log Norwegian Lutheran church was the first church in Perry and one of the earliest churches in the state. Measuring only 18 by 18 feet, the church features homemade pews of unfinished pine. The interior is unchanged, but the outside has been clapboarded over. The small pulpit and altar are combined. A small cemetery is adjacent.

For a time the building was shared by both a "high church" and a "low church" congregation. It's said the congregations grew so frustrated with each other they sometimes locked each other out of the building.

Open seven days a week for quiet meditation and memorial services, the building is on the National Register of Historic Places.

Located on Highway Z at Spring Creek Road, 1 mile north of Daleyville, Dane County.

Perry Lutheran Church, Daleyville

Perry Lutheran Church

The congregation of Perry Lutheran Church formed to follow the "high church" pattern of worship of the State Church of Norway. It had been sharing the Hauge Log Church (see above).

To follow the custom in Norway, the congregation had several annex churches, all served by Rev. Peter Marius Brodahl of Norway. At one point, Brodahl served about 20 congregations in southwestern Wisconsin.

The church was dedicated in 1861, and in 1865 the congregation officially became part of the Norwegian Synod. Brodahl served for 12 years but had disagreements with parishioners because he did not believe slavery was a sin. After he lost his wife and four of his children to disease, he returned to Norway in 1868.

In 1878 the church was heavily damaged by a tornado, which injured the pastor, Rev. Abraham Jacobson, and killed several members of the community. The church was rebuilt with the addition of a large steeple. In the 1880s, opinions split over the question of predestination (whether God predestines who will be saved or damned), causing the resignation of the Rev. Peter Isberg. In 1888 lightning struck the church's wooden steeple, and again in 1903, after which it was rebuilt in limestone and copper.

The congregation's first American-born pastor was installed in June 1910. The church was remodeled in 1915, but it burned to the ground during a thunderstorm 20 years later. It was rebuilt in 1937. Today the church is a good example of "high church" Lutheran style. The congregation is part of the Evangelical Lutheran Church in America. Regular services are held.

Located at 1057 Highway 78 south of Daleyville, Dane County, (608) 437-5294.

Koshkonong Prairie Lutheran Churches

The early Norwegian Lutherans in Dane County were happy to farm the rich land of the Koshkonong Prairie. Although they sometimes referred to the land as Karskeland, these immigrant farmers kept the Native American name for their first churches-a fairly uncommon practice. In 1844, the first Lutheran congregation was founded in the area.

First Koshkonong Lutheran Church, near Cambridge

First Koshkonong Lutheran Church was built without written plans. It has a unique and unusual architecture, with a massive crucifix serving as the main beams of the church. The interior carries the pleasant aura from the outside. At the same time, another log church was built a few miles to the west and was the beginning of West Koshkonong Church.

The steady flow of Norwegian immigrants made Koshkonong prosperous in both church and community, earning the title "Queen of Norwegian Settlements in America." In 1870, Koshkonong was the largest single parish in the Norwegian Lutheran Church with more than 4,000 members in the several congregations.

A Norwegian-born minister, Rev. Johannes Dietrichson, served the churches. In the 1850s, both churches built their first small stone structures. In the 1880s, the region experienced the internal theological conflicts of the Norwegian Synod. New churches were built within a few yards of the original churches by the 1890s.

For a time there were four Koshkonong churches in eastern Dane County. First Koshkonong and East Koshkonong were set only a few yards apart on the same side of the road. West Koshkonong and Western Koshkonong were about equally close to each other but on opposite sides of the road. By 1917, First and East Koshkonong congregations remerged into a single congregation with two buildings. West and Western Koshkonong still are separate congregations. Regular services are held.

These churches are among the most attractive in the state and located in beautiful eastern Dane County.

East Koshkonong Lutheran Church is located 4.5 miles southwest of Cambridge, east of Highway 73 on East Church Road near Hillside Road, Dane County. The interior of First Koshkonong Church can be seen by appointment and on special occasions, (608) 423-3017.

West and Western Koshkonong Lutheran Churches are located northeast of Stoughton, at 1911 Koshkonong Road, Dane County, (608) 873-9456.

York Memorial Church and Old York Church

York Memorial Church draws worshippers from Dane, Iowa, Green, and Lafayette Counties. York Church was organized in 1855, and the church building was erected in 1872. Disagreement over which synod to belong to (either the Norwegian-Danish Conference or the Norwegian Synod) caused some of the congregation to move across the road, building New York Church by 1884, which became York Memorial Church in 1952. Old York was finally torn down in 1977. A cemetery and monument still exist from the old church. Regular services are held.

Located at N9704 Highway 78, northeast of Blanchardville, Dane County, (608) 523-4239.

Yellowstone Lutheran Church

You have to follow some winding back roads to find this beautiful stone church built by Norwegian immigrants in 1868. Fayette, one of the earliest settlements in Lafayette County, was once a stop on the Monroe–Mineral Point Stage Coach line. Open Sunday mornings or by appointment. Regular services are held.

*Located at 4472 Saints Road (at the intersection with Church Road),
5 miles northwest of Argyle, Lafayette County. West from Blanchardville,
follow the signs on County F, (608) 542-4465 or 543-3088.*

A Pioneering Lutheran

The Reverend Johannes Wilhelm Christian Dietrickson came to America from Norway in the nineteenth century "prompted by the holy Biblical Word" to maintain people in the Lutheran faith. He founded many of the churches in what is now Luther Valley. He conducted his first service in 1844 at Koshkonong Prairie. Dietrickson and his churches were part of the first real synod apart from the State Church of Norway, known as the Norwegian Evangelical Lutheran Synod, founded in Luther Valley, Wisconsin, in 1851. Most of the churches are now part of the Evangelical Lutheran Church in America.

East Wiota Lutheran Church

The oldest Norwegian Lutheran Church in North America still in use, this limestone church is on the opposite side of Lafayette County from New Diggings, where there is historic St. Augustine and the Masonic Cemetery. Founded by Norwegian immigrants in 1844, the church building was erected in 1847. It is open for services every third Sunday or by appointment. On the hill in front of the church is a very large cruciform hedge. It is hard to miss the hill.

Located at 10311 Highway 78, east of Wiota,
Lafayette County, (608) 968-3328 (Wiota Lutheran Church).

Vermont Lutheran Church

Vermont Lutheran Church has changed synodal affiliations several times between the mid-1800s and the mid-1900s. It did not formally become a member of any synod until 1867, when it joined the Norwegian Synod. In 1961, American Lutheran Church, American Evangelical Church, and the Evangelical Lutheran Church combined to form the American Lutheran Church, of which Vermont Lutheran Church is a member.

The congregation has also seen several different buildings. The original was built in the 1860s on top of the hill. A new building was erected in 1909. Regular services are held.

Located at 9886 Vermont Church Road,
between Black Earth and Mount Horeb, Dane County,
(608) 767-3312 or 767-2247.

Halfway Creek Lutheran Church

This beautiful historic church, built in 1856, is on the National Register of Historic Places.

Located at W6016 County W, 2.5 miles east of Holmen,
off County D, La Crosse County, (608) 526-3701.

Coon Valley Lutherans

Three Lutheran congregations in Vernon, Monroe, and La Crosse Counties are connected and have historic significance. Coon Valley was one of the largest Norwegian settlements in America. There were no churches for about 10 years after the first settlers came to these beautiful hills. Norwegian Lutheran Congregation of Coon Valley was incorporated in July 1854, and the first church was built in 1857. This became known as Upper Coon Church in Christiana Township. Mid-Coon Church in Coon Township and Lower Coon Church in Harmony Township are two of the oldest churches in western Wisconsin, both built in 1859.

Norwegian Lutheran Congregation of Coon Valley
is located at 1005 Central Avenue (County P) at Highway 14/61,
Coon Valley, Vernon County, (608) 452-3772.

Catholic Sites

Dickeyville Grotto

One of the best-known grottoes anywhere, Dickeyville Grotto is actually a series of grottoes. It was a labor of love by Reverend Matthias Wernerus, ordained in 1907, who began the job with money he had saved from selling chickens.

Dickeyville Grotto is made of ordinary items—shells, marbles, colored glass, stones, pieces of broken china, wasps' nests—all mixed to form extraordinary "embellished concrete." It's a captivating place for adults and children alike and can be viewed in a short time or over several hours. Wernerus worked on the grotto from 1919 to 1930, including a sacred heart shrine, a patriotic shrine, and a Corpus Christi altar, among many other features. The grotto was restored in 1995 and 1996.

Each year, an estimated 60,000 pilgrims visit the grotto, which is open year-round. Guided tours are held from 9 a.m. to 6 p.m., April 15 through October.

There is no cost, but donations are accepted. A large gift shop is open from 9 a.m. to 6 p.m. seven days a week, April 1 to October 31.

Wernerus's grave is nearby, featuring stones from holy lands and Ojibwe arrowheads and axes. Regular services are held at Holy Ghost Parish.

Located on Highway 34/61, Dickeyville, Grant County, (608) 568-3119. Holy Ghost Parish, (608) 568-7519. netcolony.com/pets/agilitynut/dickeyville.htm; dickeyville platteville.wi.us/visitors/grotto.html

Holy Family Grotto, near La Crosse

Holy Family Grotto

Fathers Paul Dobberstein, Matt Szerencse, and Frank Donsky built this grotto between 1925 and 1930. It is visible from St. Joseph Road on the grounds of Villa St. Joseph, a retirement community of the Franciscan Sisters of Perpetual Adoration. Viewing times are Monday through Saturday, 9 to 11 a.m., and 1 to 3:30 p.m. and Sunday from 1 to 3:30 p.m.

Located on Highway 33, St. Joseph, 10 miles east of La Crosse, La Crosse County, (608) 788-5100.

The Plain Shrine at St. Anne's Hill

Visiting the Plain Shrine dedicated to St. Anne is a true pilgrimage, because it's not an easy place to reach. The visitor must pass through a cow pasture (and close the gate behind, to keep the cows from escaping) and then walk to the top of Council Bluff—quite a climb. The beautiful little stone chapel atop the hill is worth the effort.

The Plain Shrine and its altar are built of fossil stone, with windows export-ed from Trevis, Germany. It took five years to build and was opened in 1928. The building material includes broken glass from the windows of nearby St. Luke's church, destroyed by a tornado in 1918.

The path to the shrine starts at Reservoir and Oak Streets, where one will find the first of the Stations of the Cross. Follow the stations and you wind up, breathless, at the top of Council Bluff, which was used by Native Americans as a place from which to send smoke signals. The Stations of the Cross were donated by Holy Hill after new stations were installed there.

The Pilgrim's Prayer on display there reads in part: "Many pilgrims coming to this place have felt the effects of your kindness and powerful intercession. Gladly have I traveled to this holy place to seek your favor. I have every hope that you will be gracious to me as you have been to all who came here with faith and in hope."

St. Luke's Catholic Church, to which the shrine belongs, began in 1857 with 12 families. The current church, dedicated in 1940, serves 470 households.

The church is located at 1240 Nachreiner Avenue, off Highway 23, Plain, Sauk County. The shrine is accessible by starting the Stations of the Cross at Reservoir and Oak Streets, (608) 546-2482.

Our Lady of Sorrows Chapel and Gate of Heaven Cemetary

Founded in 1891, the Catholic cemetery is on the National Register of Historic Places. There are three remaining grottoes dated 1883–1916, 14 Stations of the Cross, and many beautiful statues. Our Lady of Sorrows, also called Holy Cross Chapel, is a small precious chapel located in the middle of the cemetery.

Located at 519 Losey Boulevard, La Crosse, La Crosse County, (608) 782-0238.

Queen of the Holy Rosary Mediatrix Peace Shrine

In 1949, Mary Ann Van Hoof, housewife and mother of seven, reported seeing and hearing an apparition of the Virgin Mary. The fact that the Roman Catholic Church has never recognized her vision didn't stop pilgrims from flocking to the area. On August 15, 1950, 100,000 people gathered there to await another vision, turning Necedah into Wisconsin's answer to Fatima.

Today a large gift shop, a series of dioramas, and a loudspeaker system playing hymns mark the site where Mary is said to have visited Van Hoof many times over a 30-year period and given her messages about sexual morality, abortion, and the evils of Communism.

There is an elementary school at the site, and a large "House of Prayer" is also under construction. A semi-Catholic organization, For God and My Country, was founded around the shrine (the Church of Rome has condemned the shrine and ordered it closed). The organization does not recognize Vatican II and speaks out against modern changes in the Church. The group is probably most closely aligned with the Old Catholics.

Female visitors to the shrine are told to "dress Mary-like" and must wear long dresses or skirts. For those who show up in shorts or pants, wrap-around skirts are available to borrow. Says a sign at the door: "Clothing should conceal, not reveal. . . . History reveals that when the morals of a nation collapse, the nation collapses!"

The shrine is open 24 hours a day.

Located at W5703 Shrine Road and East 22nd Street, Necedah, Juneau County. From I-90/94, take Highway 80 to Necedah, (608) 565-2617.

Schoenstatt Heights, Founder's Shrine

The first Schoenstatt Shrine Chapel to be built in the United States, the "Founder's Shrine" was dedicated on June 20, 1953. Bishop O'Connor, the first bishop of the Madison Diocese invited the Schoenstatt sisters to Wisconsin.

Schoenstatt Heights is also a small retreat center with a large conference hall. Reservations are required for personal and/or individual retreats. For more information on the Schoenstatt Order and its other shrines, see chapter 2.

Located at 3601 Cottage Grove Road (County BB) on the edge of Madison's east side, Dane County, (608) 222-7280. schsrsmary.org

Our Lady of the Fields Shrine

Built 1903 and dedicated 1910, this small shrine church was rededicated to Our Lady of the Fields in 1958 by Bishop William O'Connor. The chapel seats about 60. It is a fairly popular rural place for pilgrimage and stands on a hill, where one can see as far as Blue Mounds.

Located at E3694 Chapel Road, about 7 miles north of Plain and just northwest of White Mound County Park, Sauk County. From either Highway 130 or Highway 23, take County N to County G north to the shrine and cemetery. ohwy.com/wi/b/blumousp.htm

Our Lady of Guadalupe National Shrine

A work in progress that was begun in 2000, this shrine is expected to be a pilgrimage as popular as Holy Hill, drawing visitors from around the country. The large $25 million center, set on a high bluff overlooking the Mississippi River, will serve western Wisconsin and will feature a center for "doctrinal and spiritual renewal."

Located just off Highway 35 south of La Crosse, La Crosse County.

Mazzuchelli Churches

Rev. Samuel Mazzuchelli was born in 1806 in Italy, the 15th of 16 children. He came to America to work with Native Americans, settlers, and miners. This missionary, architect, and founder of the Dominican Sisters mother house, Sinsinawa, built 25 churches and eight public buildings and established nine schools. In 1832, Father Mazzuchelli traveled on horseback to "bring people who had given up their religion back to the church." He has been beatified by the Vatican, which is the second stage for recognition as an official saint of the Roman Catholic Church.

Father Mazzuchelli would ride on horseback from town to town, celebrating Mass in log cabins and bringing wayward Catholics back to the church. He wrote catechisms in the Ho-Chunk (Winnebago) language and an almanac in Ojibwe. Father Mazzuchelli died of pneumonia in 1864 in Benton, Wisconsin, where he is buried behind St. Patrick's Catholic Church. The process for beatification was opened in Rome in 1967. Pope John XXIII called him "the herald of the Gospel" in the tri-state area.

The Mazzuchelli Exhibit at Sinsinawa Mound traces his life; large groups are asked to call ahead at (608) 748-4411.

Interestingly, the stone **St. Patrick's Catholic Church** was built around an existing wooden church, and services continued to be held in the old structure until the new building was completed. The church celebrated its 150-year anniversary in 1999. A plaque in the cemetery where Father Mazzuchelli is buried says, "A Catholic Cemetery is a sacred place because it is the final resting place for the body which is the temple of the Holy Spirit until it is reunited with the soul at resurrection." His grave has become a place of pilgrimage. Located on County J (at Highway 11), Benton, Lafayette County, (608) 759-2131.

St. Matthew's Catholic Church,
Shullsburg

155

The log mission church of St Paul's Parish began in 1838, organized by Father Mazzuchelli. Mission Church families in Mineral Point worshiped in homes until Rock Church (St. Paul's) was built in 1842, the third oldest church in Wisconsin. Many of the original furnishings are still there, including Father Mazzuchelli's altar stone. In 1854, a larger church was built, and then a third church was built in the early 1900s. The Rock Church, a simple one-story limestone building, is open during Mineral Point's Tour of Homes every summer or by appointment by calling (608) 987-3361. The building is on the National Register of Historic Places. The congregation's present building was built in 1911 and is next door to St. Paul's Mission Church, located at 411 Ridge Street (Highway 151), (608) 787-2026.

The oldest of the Mazzuchelli churches is **St. Augustine Church**, a wooden structure built in 1844 in the Greek Revival style. An annual mass is held there the last Sunday in September at 2:30 p.m. The church is open Sunday 1 to 4 p.m., May 31 through September 30, or by appointment; call (608) 744-3438 (Shullsburg) or (608) 854-2396 (Hazel Green). St. Augustine's is up the road from County W, New Diggings, Lafayette County.

St. Thomas Parish, founded in 1838, features a beautiful little garden for meditation. A sign reminds visitors to "Remember God loves you more than you will ever know or imagine" (attributed to Father Richard J. Leffler). Located at 101 Church Street, Potosi Grant County. madisondiocese.org/tennyson

St. Andrew Parish, founded in 1846, was built in 1875 and features an ornately carved altar and an unusual Virgin Mary grotto with a rose on her foot. The same pastor serves both St. Thomas and St. Andrew parishes. Located in Tennyson, Grant County, (608) 763-2671. madisondiocese.org/tennyson

St. Matthew's Catholic Church, built in 1861 is still in use. Through Father Mazzuchelli's influence, most of the town's street names have religious significance. For instance, the church is located at the corner of Truth and Judgment Streets in Shullsburg, Lafayette County, (608) 965-4518.

St. Gabriel Catholic Church is considered to be the oldest church in the state. Father Lucien Galter, pastor of St. Gabriel's from 1847 to 1866 and founder of St. Paul, Minnesota, is entombed in front of this church. Located at 506 Beaumont, Prairie du Chien, Crawford County, (608) 326-2404.

Also see the nearby listing for Sinsinawa Mound Convent and Retreat Center.

Sinsinawa Mound Convent and Retreat Center

Sinsinawa is Algonquin for "rattlesnake," and there is a rattlesnake effigy mound in the area. In Sioux, the word means "home of the young eagle." The area around Sinsinawa Mound was called "Manitoumie," which means "land where the spirit dwells."

The institution was founded in 1844, when Father Samuel Mazzuchelli built a college and started the Dominican Sisters. Edgewood College in Madison is a branch of Sinsinawa. The convent features an unusual modern chapel and a gallery with relics of the saints set into modern art. A unique labyrinth is made of brick and stone. A large bookshop carries a variety of spiritual and religious literature and gifts.

A wide assortment of conferences and programs are available. The facility's mission statement reads, in part, "Sinsinawa Mound is a center of Dominican Life and mission committed to developing, renewing, and celebrating the interrelationship of all creation. Its hallmarks are spirituality, community, hospitality, education, and earth stewardship."

The retreat center features a 750-seat auditorium, 135 single bedrooms, and two small suites with kitchenettes. Costs vary. Weekend guided retreats are available.

Located in Sinsinawa on County Z between Hazel Green in Grant County and Dubuque, Iowa, (608) 748-4411. sinsinawa.org/smc.htm

Durward's Glen

This beautiful glen was formed 10,000 years ago at the end of the Wisconsin Ice Age by water melting from the great glaciers. The Catholic retreat and monastery was founded in 1862 by the Order of Camillus. It provides a serene place for prayer and meditation, and a sign requests silence.

The 110-acre Durward's Glen features an outside Holy Family altar, used for outdoor mass. The Italian sculpture is unusual in that it portrays Jesus as a child. There is also a wooden Stations of the Cross. On the east bank of the glen, Charles Durward carved a Maltese cross in the 1860s.

Considered a "Center for Spiritual Healing," the retreat offers programs on topics including grieving, nature, money insecurity, and Christian beliefs. A new, additional site with a retreat building is located a quarter mile up the street. The site is on the National Register of Historic Places.

Located at W1187 McLeisch Road (off Highway 78), about 8 miles southeast of Baraboo, Columbia County, (608) 356-8113 or (608) 356-4523.

Camp Gray

Operated by the Catholic Diocese of Madison, Camp Gray has been in operation for more than 40 years. The 225-acre camp features an outdoor chapel built by campers, a sacred fire pit, a large retreat center, a bunkhouse, and cabins with and without electric power. According to the camp's mission statement, "Camp Gray, a ministry of the Catholic Diocese of Madison, offers a natural sanctuary to people of all faiths to discover self, experience God, and walk hand in hand with friends."

Programs provide camping "with a spiritual emphasis," and themes include confirmation, "True Love Waits," Christian community, and an environmental stewardship program. Weekends, day camp, and overnights are available. There are special programs for deaf and disabled children, as well as opportunities for low-income families.

"We will reinforce the Christian values you are teaching in your home," says Phil DeLong, director. "We create a safe place for your kids to grow in relationship with God, self, and others, to make decisions, to learn new skills, to become more confident and more well-rounded individuals."

Lodging prices vary. Reservations can be made up to a year in advance. The American Camping Association accredits the camp.

Located near Mirror Lake State Park
on E10213 Shady Lane Road, Reedsburg,
Sauk County, (608) 356-8200. campgray.com

Maria Angelorum Chapel

Every moment since August 1, 1878, at least two nuns have maintained a 24-hour prayer vigil for the La Crosse community, the church, the city, and the world at the **Perpetual Adoration Chapel** connected to the beautiful Maria Angelorum ("Mary of the Angels") Chapel. The Franciscan Sisters take one-hour shifts at the gold and white altar.

Maria Angelorum features Corinthian pillars and simulated Norwegian marble columns. There is a Casavant pipe organ with 1,422 pipes and more than 100 windows of Bavarian stained glass, each featuring a different angel.

St. Rose Convent is a motherhouse that has been in continuous use by the Franciscan Sisters of Perpetual Adoration for more than a century. Because of its awe-inspiring chapels, it is one of the most popular visitor sites in La Crosse.

These same sisters founded the surrounding **Viterbo College** in 1890. The liberal arts college is located at 815 South Ninth Street.

Altar of the Maria Angelorum Chapel, La Crosse

They also operate the **Franciscan Spirituality Center**. The facilities offer a number of services including retreats and workshops of special interest to women.

Located at 715 South Ninth Street, at Market Street, La Crosse, La Crosse County.
Visitors are asked to call (608) 791-5295 before visiting. fspa.org

St. Benedict Center Monastery

The Catholic monastery opened in 1953, and the Benedictine sisters established the ecumenical retreat and conference center in 1966. The retreat center is on 130 acres overlooking Lake Mendota, providing a serene and tranquil setting for meetings. The monastery has 17 bedrooms, some double and some single, all with private baths. Cost varies; spiritual guidance is offered for $30.

The lower monastery building was renovated and allows for private retreats.

Located at 4600 Highway M, on the north side of Lake Mendota,
Middleton, Dane County, (608) 836-1631. sbcenter.org

St. Norbert House

In 1845, Norbertine missionary Father Adalbert Inama of Austria came to Dane County. The first Catholic priest in the area, he founded the first Catholic church in the county and was thus known as "Father of the Catholic Faith" in northwest Dane County. He erected a log cabin one mile from the current yellow stone church. He served seven counties: Dane, Iowa, Columbia, Dodge, Jefferson, Sauk, and Waukesha, and "read Mass" in the assembly chamber of the state capitol building.

St. Norbert Church in Roxbury opened in 1853. A painting of a Raphaelite Madonna hangs above the high altar. Visitors are encouraged to visit during Mass. Group tours can be arranged by contacting the Sauk Prairie Area Historical Society.

Located at 8944 County Y, west of County KP,
east of Highway 12/19, Roxbury, Dane County,
(608) 643-3661. madisondiocese.org/roxbury

Solitude Ridge Hermitages

Sponsored by the Franciscan Sisters of Perpetual Adoration in La Crosse on the sister's Villa St. Joseph Property, these three individual hermitages are available for retreat. The literature refers to it as "a place of solitude. It is a sacred space where the wisdom, beauty, and goodness of God are present in all of nature." The cost is a deposit of $20 and $25 per night or $150 per week. It is open year-round. A six-day retreat is available; visitors must prepare their own food.

Located in the village of St. Joseph, La Crosse County.
Make reservations by calling the Franciscan Spirituality Center
in La Crosse, (608) 791-5295.

Cathedral of St. Joseph the Workman

This beautiful modern cathedral receives visitors and pilgrims from all over the world. The building was dedicated in 1962 by the Mother Church of Diocese of La Crosse on the site of the old Cathedral of St. Joseph built in 1869.

With a seating capacity 1,072, the church offers three Masses each weekday and five Masses on Sundays. Professor Anton Wendling of Germany designed the great window, *Tree of Life*. The rest of the windows are by Leo Cartright of England. The giant pipe organ contains more than 4,200 pipes. The ceiling features four-foot-square gold leaf panels with Celtic designs.

Outdoors, a sculpture, *Common Cloth*, was created in 1993 by Robert Leverich, dedicated to laborers and their connection to God. Regular services are held.

Located at 530 Main Street, La Crosse, La Crosse County,
(608) 782-0322. cathedralsjworkman.org

St. Raphael Cathedral

Built on land donated to the Catholic Church by Governor James Doty in 1848, the cornerstone for the cathedral was laid in 1854, and the building was ready for use in 1862. It was the first Catholic church in Madison and became the diocesan cathedral when the 11-county Madison Diocese was founded in 1946. Regular services are held.

Located at 222 W. Main Street,
Madison, Dane County, (608) 256-5614.

St. Mary of the Oaks Chapel, near Mazomanie

St. Mary of the Oaks Chapel

This tiny stone chapel was built in 1857 by John Endres to give thanks to God for sparing his family from diphtheria. He built the chapel at the highest point of a steep incline in northwestern Dane County. Literally tons of rocks had to be dragged to the site by oxen. The 18-inch-thick walls reflect the building methods of German settlers. The rounded apse is a Germanic-style wonder. Archbishop Sebastian Messmer of Milwaukee dedicated the chapel in 1926.

Located in Indian Lake County Park, on Highway 19 between Mazomanie and Springfield Corners, Dane County.

St. Mary's Ridge Church

The view of this church is the official U. S. Department of Agriculture Midwest farm scene displayed in Washington D.C. and the Corn Palace in Mitchell, South Dakota. The massive yellow cream brick building, built in 1897, overlooks a valley.

Located on County U, about midway between Cashton and Norwalk, Monroe County, (608) 823-7906.

SS Anthony and Phillip Parish

The congregation formed in 1846, and the building was erected in 1869. Its two steeples can be seen from a distance. The impressive large church building is worth the ride up the hill. Regular services are held.

Located at 726 Main Street (Highway 80) across from Highland Park, Highland, Iowa County, (608) 929-7490. madisondiocese.org/highland/

St. Patrick's Parish

Built in 1964 and shaped like a circle, this church was one of the first designed with the altar in the center—a development made possible with the changes of Vatican II. St. Patrick's was established in 1886. Another Irish Catholic church in Lodi, St. Kiernan's (established in 1857) was dissolved in 1894; its members eventually joined St. Patrick's.

Located at 521 Farr Street, Lodi, Columbia County, (608) 592-5711.

St. Barnabas Church

The first church in the Mazomanie–Black Earth area was a log church built in 1862. The stone building was built in 1890. Then a fire gutted the church and destroyed the steeple in 1929. Reconstruction and renovation developed the remarkable and massive hammer-beam ceiling—making it unique in the Madison Diocese. Regular services are held.

Located at 410 Cramer, one block off Highway 14, Mazomanie, Dane County, (608) 795-4321.

Holy Redeemer Mission Church

With a congregation of German Catholic settlers that goes back to 1846, Holy Redeemer erected its first building in 1861, two years after one parishioner had to walk 26 miles to Madison to find a priest to administer last rites. The current church was built in 1916 with a stone shrine altar for Corpus Christi observance.

Parishioner Mary M. Suter said, "It was once written that this early pioneer church was a haven, a place of sanctuary, where the early immigrants could find and develop their best selves." Regular services are held.

Located on Spring Valley Road about 6 miles southwest of Mount Vernon, Dane County, (608) 437-5884.

St. John the Evangelist Church

William Wesley Peters of Taliesin Architects, considered Frank Lloyd Wright's best student, designed this church. The design includes a great deal of iconography.

The congregation dates to 1857 when many Catholic families came to the area to work on the railroad. A new church was built after a fire destroyed the old church in 1988, just after an extensive renovation for Vatican II. Many of the icons are from David Giffey, a Madison iconographer. Today there are 458 families in the parish. Regular services are held.

Located at 253 N. Washington Street (entrance is on Daley Street between Washington and Lexington Streets), Spring Green, Iowa County, (608) 588-2028.
madisondiocese.org/springgreen

Bishop O'Connor Pastoral Center (Holy Name Seminary)

The Pastoral Center is named for the first Bishop of the Madison Diocese. After Bishop William Bullock closed Holy Name Seminary in 1995, he began the process of renovating the facilities and developing shrines for the main chapel. One is dedicated to Father Samuel Mazzuchelli, another to Mother Teresa of Calcutta. The center has room for retreats and conferences.

Located at 3577 High Point Road, Madison, Dane County, (608) 821-3130.

*M*ethodist Sites
Welsh Calvinistic Methodist Church

Built in 1859, the Welsh Calvinistic Methodist Church may be the oldest church building in La Crosse County. Welsh Calvinists held services there until 1916. In 1920, they assimilated into the Presbyterian Church. The building is now vacant.

Located at 504 Commercial Street, Bangor, La Crosse County.
First Presbyterian Church of Bangor, (608) 486-2670.

First Methodist Episcopal Church

Methodists were the first Christian group to settle in Baraboo Valley. The Methodist Episcopal Society erected the first church in Baraboo in 1830 at the very site of the current church. The current and larger church was built in 1853. An 1899 fire required some rebuilding that was completed the same year.

Located at 615 Broadway Street, at Fifth Street, Baraboo, Sauk County, (608) 356-3991.

Pleasant Ridge Cemetery

The African-American community of Pleasant Ridge had its origins in the 1840s when William Horner of Virginia brought his former slaves, the Shepard family, to the site. By the 1880s the area was home to more than 100 free or escaped slaves. At one point the area had a church and a school. Now the cemetery on a scenic ridge top is all that remains.

The nearby community of Beetown built the United Brethren Methodist Church in 1882, which was shared by whites and blacks.

Pleasant Ridge Cemetery and memorial marker are located on Slab Town Road,
north of Highway 35/81, between Beetown and Lancaster, Grant County,
(608) 723-7772 (Lancaster United Methodist Church).

Willerup United Methodist Church

Dating to 1851, this was the first Scandinavian Methodist church anywhere in the world. The church is an early Gothic Revival style. Christian Willerup, a former Lutheran, founded the church in 1832. Regular services are held.

Located at 414 W. Water Street, Cambridge, Dane County,
(608) 423-3777. wisconsinumc.org/cambridge_willerupumc

Linden Methodist Church, Linden

Linden Methodist Church

Cornish immigrants built this stone church to resemble churches from home. Visitors can view the church during Sunday services, or they can pick up a key at the nearby Corner Store. Built in 1851, the building is on the National Register of Historic Places. Regular services are held.

Located on Highway 39 (at Main and Church Streets), Linden, Iowa County, (608) 623-2525.

Primitive Methodist Church

This tiny stone Cornish church from 1861, with a collection of similar stone buildings, has an unusual stone fence along the road and cemetery. These buildings and walls are all that is left of the mining village that was settled in 1837. Homecoming services are held the last Sunday in June.

Located 4 miles north of Benton on Carr Factory Road, Jenkynsville, Lafayette County, (608) 744-2202.

Roundtree-Mitchell Cottage

Dating to the 1830s, the building is a "Historic shrine to American freedom and experimental Christianity." This was an early meeting place for Methodists in the state.

Located on the northeast corner of Jewett and Lancaster Streets, off Highway 81, Platteville, Grant County, (608) 723-2287.

Hyde Chapel (Union Congregational Church)

This Welsh Methodist church, an example of Greek Revival style, was built in 1862 and shared by English and Welch worshippers. The congregation was founded in the 1830s. The chapel, which seats about 60, is on the National Register of Historic Places. A marker says the chapel is "in loving memory of the pioneers who provided a place of worship and of rest." Regular services are held.

Located at Hyde's Mills, County H, Ridgeway, Iowa County, (608) 753-2283.

Rutland Church
and Cemetery,
Rutland

Rutland Church

The Rutland Church was once the cradle of the United Brethren Conference, which merged with the United Methodist Church in 1969. Congregational activity in the area dates back to 1840. The building was erected in 1852, the first United Brethren church in the state. The first session of the Wisconsin Conference of the United Brethren was held here in September of 1858. Services were held in the building until 1912.

Located on Old Stone Road at Highway 14 in Rutland, Dane County.
oregon.k12.wi.us/webpages/orpages/RutlandUnited.html

Wyoming Methodist Church

This church began as a Presbyterian church, later became a Congregational church and then a Methodist church in 1903. The building, erected in 1851, is eligible for listing in the National Register of Historic Places.

Located south of Spring Green, on Highway 23 at
Lower Wyoming Valley Road, Wyoming, Iowa County, (608) 588-2837.

*P*resbyterian Sites

Oakland Cambridge Presbyterian Church

With a congregation that formed in 1846, the current building was started with a cornerstone laid in 1888. Completed in 1889, the church has had three separate renovations, mostly to the interior. It remains active as "a friendly church by the side of the road." Regular services are held.

Located at 313 Main Street (Highway 12) at North Street, Cambridge, on the Dane/Jefferson County border, (608) 423-3001. smallbytes.net/ocpres/

Carmel Presbyterian Church, Rewey

Carmel Presbyterian Church

The man who may have been the world's only self-proclaimed "Welsh Negro," James D. Williams, was born a slave in Virginia and made free by President Abraham Lincoln's Emancipation Proclamation. After Williams's death in 1903, he was laid to rest beside the former Welsh Calvinistic Methodist Church, of which he was an esteemed member and where he sang in the church choir.

"Negro Jim," as he was known, came to Wisconsin with members of the Pecatonica Welsh community who had fought in the Civil War. Most of the community welcomed him. Williams owned his own lead mine, three miles south of Rewey.

Today the building still contains only its wood-burning stove for heat, so it is used only in the summer. In the winter, congregants use the newer Carmel-Peniel Presbyterian Church building for worship.

Located on County A, near Rewey, on the western edge of Iowa County.

Episcopal Sites

Grace Episcopal Church

Originally called "The Apostolic Church," what is now Grace Episcopal Church was organized in 1838, when Bishop Jackson Kemper conducted the first Episcopal service in Madison. The only Episcopal Church in Madison for nearly 70 years, Grace had grown to 450 members by 1858.

The present building, a Madison landmark, was dedicated in 1858. In its nave are a dozen large stained glass windows of unusual beauty, installed between 1887 and 1957, illustrating the birth, death, resurrection, and continuing ministry of Christ. The church's famous baptistery window is at the rear of left aisle of nave, installed by Tiffany Art Glass Studio in 1899. The church literature says stained glass has always been important to bring "color into the lives of people and making each worshipper see God as the source of light, color, and beauty." Madison's first pipe organ was dedicated to Grace during Easter 1869 (the current organ was installed in the late 1980s).

In 1940s Grace was one of the first churches in the country to move the altar forward so clergy could face the congregation. In 1979 it opened its food pantry, which now serves a thousand people a month. The church's homeless shelter houses 60 to 110 men every night.

The sandstone building, on the National Register of Historic Places, is the only remaining church of the four that were originally built on the Capital Square in the 1800s. Regular services are held.

Located at 116 W. Washington Avenue, Madison, Dane County, (608) 255-5147.

Trinity Church

Trinity Church is the fifth oldest Episcopal parish in Wisconsin. Its first service was held in 1838, and it was officially organized in 1845. The territory's first Governor, Henry Dodge, was a member. The First Methodist Episcopal Church, erected in 1867, is across the street. Regular services are held.

Located at 409 High Street (on the corner of North Iowa and High Streets), one block off Highway 151, Mineral Point, Grant County, (608) 987-3019.

Christ Church of La Crosse

This large, impressive red sandstone church is on the National Register of Historic Places. It was built in 1897. The parish traces its origins to 1850 when the first complete service of Christian Divine Worship in La Crosse was conducted on Granddad's Bluff. The 1975 commemorative marker at the top of the bluff indicates that Reverend Father James Lloyd Breck was the celebrant, with "his company of pioneer missionaries" of Holy Eucharist according to the Book of Common Prayer, on June 23, 1850. Regular services are held.

Located at 111 Ninth Street, La Crosse, La Crosse County,
(800) 688-9424 or (608) 784-0697.

St John the Baptist Church

In 1836, the first Episcopal service was celebrated in Portage, but there was not a parish until 1855. A beautiful meditation garden is open to the public year-round. Regular services are held.

Located at 211 W. Pleasant Street, Portage, Columbia County,
(608) 742-6054. centurytel.net/sjtb

Holy Trinity Church

This simple brown wood-paneled building is the second oldest Episcopal parish in Wisconsin, dating back to the military chaplaincy at Fort Crawford. The current building was built in 1854 on land purchased by Wisconsin's first Episcopal bishop, Bishop Kemper. Regular services are held.

Located between Highways 18 and 35 at 220 Michigan Street, Prairie du Chien, Crawford
County, (608) 326-6085.

Eastern Orthodox Sites

St. Nicholas Chapel at
St. Isaac of Syria Russian
Orthodox Skete,
near Boscobel

St. Isaac of Syria Russian Orthodox Skete

Founded in 1987, the residents of this small Russian Orthodox skete and convent support themselves by producing a large percentage of the icons to be found in North America. Visitors are welcome but are asked to call first.

Located on Spring Valley Road, off Highway 61, northwest of Boscobel, Crawford County,
(608) 375-5500 or (800) 81ICONS. nettinker.com/monasteries/isaac.htm, skete.com

St. Elias Antiochian Church

The first Orthodox church in the state that was not either Russian or Greek, St. Elias Antiochian was founded in 1909. The 1917 building is also a historic site for the city of La Crosse. Regular services are held.

Located at 710 Copeland Avenue, La Crosse,
La Crosse County, (608) 782-8641.
antiochian.org/midwest/Parishes/St_Elias_LaCrosse.htm

Assumption Greek Orthodox Church

Unique for its internationally known fresco icons painted by local iconographer David Giffey, Assumption Greek Orthodox Church was incorporated in 1951. The current church building is a former Methodist church building built in the 1930s that was renovated in the late 1970s; a dome, sanctuary, and transepts were added, which made the building an excellent example of a traditional Greek cross-shaped church.

The dome, which symbolizes heaven, features the image of the Pantocratora (Jesus Christ the All-Powerful). Along the walls of the sanctuary are icons of church fathers. Other icons include the Mother of God, the four evangelists, the ascension of Jesus, and a variety of Bible figures. A booklet is available that describes the wall-to-wall icons and their meanings. The iconography work has continued, and the interior of the church has seen several improvements and renovations. The community has about 184 families from various ethnic backgrounds. Regular services are held.

Located at 11 N. Seventh Street, Madison, Dane County,
(608) 244-1001. assumptionmadison.org/main.html

Other Christian Sites

Chapel in the Pines

Voted the "best hidden wonder" in 1998 by readers of a local newspaper, the *News-Sickle-Arrow*, this cozy little log chapel surrounded by woods seats only about 10 worshippers. It is associated with the Arena Congregational Church. The site is a memorial for Bill Akins (1948–1998) and is a town park.

Located off Highway 14 on Reimann Road, across from the Arena Cheese Factory Outlet, Arena, Iowa County, (608) 753-2271. madison.tec.wi.us/ia/ae/cyero/chapelpines.htm

Freda Meyers Nishan Memorial Chapel

This chapel was built of local stones for use by any denomination. The building measures 31 by 60 feet with a southern wing of 19 by 28 feet. The outline is a broken ashlar design, and an open truss roof domes the chapel. A spire in the southwest corner of the building makes it visible from a distance. There are four crypts in the basement.

Located in Greenwood Cemetery, just north of Reedsburg on County K, Sauk County.

Boscobel Central Hotel

Anyone who has ever been in a motel is familiar with the Gideon's Bible. Boscobel Central Hotel, built in 1881, is the site of the origin of the Gideon Bible movement. One night in 1898, two salesmen were sharing a room and began discussing how as Christians they might support each other and other travelers. John H. Nicholson and Samuel E. Hill decided to start a mutual help organization recognizing Christian travelers. The first organizational meeting was held a few months later. There is an official Wisconsin historic marker at the site.

Boscobel Central Hotel, Boscobel

The room has been restored and is available for viewing on request. Room 19 has another claim to fame—it's the room where John F. and Jacqueline

Kennedy stopped to freshen up during a campaign stop in March 1960. Whether coincidentally or not, JFK junior was born nine months later.

Located at 1005 Wisconsin Avenue, Boscobel, Grant County. Make an appointment by calling (608) 375-5001 or (888) 710-5206. boscobelwisconsin.com/hotel.html

Advent Christian Church of La Valle

Organized as the Church of God in 1876 by Elder E. P. Graves, the church was united with the Advent Christian Conference in 1877. The building was finished in 1878. It is the oldest Advent Christian church in the state. Regular services are held.

Located at E3612 Jessop Road, La Valle, Sauk County, (608) 985-7374.

Seventh-Day Adventist Church of Waterloo

This church is vacant but is interesting to visit for the cemetery with Civil War-era headstones.

Located on Highway 133, south of Cassville, Grant County.

Swiss United Church of Christ

Swiss UCC calls itself "a historical church with a unique vision of the future." Its church family dates back to 1849, when the first immigrant church was built in New Glarus by early settlers from Canton Glarus, Switzerland. Today the church still celebrates Swiss Kilby (Swiss church-dedication day) the last Sunday in September. Active in the community, the church also provides a food pantry and a mission to New Glarus Nursing Home. Services vary in format but follow the central theme of Bible-based sermons. Regular services are held.

Located at First Street and Fifth Avenue, New Glarus, Green County, (608) 527-2119.

Seventh-Day Baptist Church

Seventh-Day Baptists are similar to other Baptist sects except that they celebrate the Sabbath on Saturdays. Dane County's Seventh-Day Baptist congregation was organized in 1843, and the church, a clapboard structure in the Greek Revival style, was erected in the far southeastern part of the county in 1863. A two-story addition was added to the south side in 1956. During the Civil War, the church was part of the Underground Railroad to help slaves escape to the North.

Seventh-Day Baptist Church, Albion

Albion Academy, across the square, was chartered in 1853, opened in 1854, and founded and operated by Northwestern Seventh-Day Baptist Association. In 1918 the Norwegian Evangelistic Lutheran Church of America took over. Kumlien Hall is now a historical museum. There is a Wisconsin official historic marker at the site, listing Albion Academy's outstanding students including Alva Adams (governor of Colorado), Knute Nelson (U.S. senator from Minnesota), and world-famous botanist Edwin L. Greene.

Located at 616 Albion Road (Highway 51), Albion, Dane County, (608) 884-3711.
inwave.com/churches/albionsdb/

God's Country

The phrase "God's Country" that describes western Wisconsin did not originate with the G. Heileman Brewing Company (many years a fixture in La Crosse) to sell its beer. The phrase is attributed to Rev. D.O. Van Syke, who was convinced that the La Crosse and Trempealeau County area was the biblical Garden of Eden. He thought that the region's four rivers, bluffs, hanging gardens, fruit (especially apples), milk, and honey closely matched the Bible's descriptions of paradise. As a circuit-riding preacher in the late 1800s, he promulgated his discovery of Eden to bring people back to the land of innocence—where Highway 33 and Highway 54 now meet. According to a tract written by Van Syke in 1886, he suggested that Adam and Eve left paradise for . . . Minnesota.

Valton Friends Church

The valleys around Ironton attracted "radical" sects such as Amish and Quakers. The Quaker Friends Church was founded in 1890. Some Quakers forbade crosses or steeples or any kind of planned sermons; this particular church is more similar to other Christian denominations in that it has all three. The Quakers are still distinguished by the simplicity of their worship services, which include few rituals. The Valton Friends Church now has a congregation of about 60. Regular services are held.

Located at S1939 Landsinger Road, Valton,
about 6 miles southwest of Wonewoc,
Sauk County, (608) 464-7414.

Excelsior Retreat Center

Interdenominational and interfaith, this retreat center is "dedicated to the use of all God's faithful that seek a peaceful and beautiful location." Opened in 1992 by and affiliated with the Liberal Catholic Church, the center includes space for small group retreats, seminars, workshops, conferences, training sessions, and meetings for up to 50, as well as individuals and couples. Psychotherapy workshops and holistic health retreats are also available. There are a lodge building and small cottages with electricity. The worship area includes the Chapel of St. Michael.

Located on Chitwood Hollow Road, Excelsior,
about 8 miles northeast of Boscobel,
Richland County, (608) 537-2973.

Western Wisconsin Spiritual Center

Formerly Wonewoc Spiritualist Camp, this facility was recently turned over to the National Spiritualist Association of Churches. The camp, on the grounds of ancient Native American healing grounds, is open during the summer only and closed on Mondays. The regular programs offer psychic readings, mediumship, healing, and personal retreats. Groups may be accommodated as well. Costs vary according to cabin, length of stay, type of readings, etc. The Spirit Chapel is an intimate blend of eclectic images, both Christian and pagan. There is a variety of sacred spots in the campgrounds including a sweat lodge and a healing tree in the center of the grounds. The word *wonewoc* is Ojibwe for "they howl," as the hills and bluffs would echo the call of wolves at night. It has been nicknamed "Spook Hill" by local residents of the town below.

Twenty-five cabins plus six modern hotel rooms are available for rental; 3,500 people have visited the camp each summer. It has been open to visitors for more than 100 years.

Located at 304 Hill Street, Wonewoc, Juneau County, (608) 464-7466 or (800) 850-7113. angelfire.com/biz2/wonewoc

Zarahemla, the Sacred City of God

In the 1840s, the Blanchardville Latter Day Saints named their community Zarahemla, a name taken from an 1841 revelation of Joseph Smith: "Let them build up a city unto my name upon the land opposite the city of Nauvoo, and let the name of Zarahemla be named upon it."

This was a major religious center of Mormon activity in southwest Wisconsin, especially for the Reorganized church. The community goes back to the 1840s and William Cline and Samuel Horner (both Latter Day Saints), who acquired land along the Pecatonica River, the present site of Blanchardville. Except for Native Americans and squatters, the region was untouched by "Gentiles" (non-Mormons), so it was believed that modern Israel could establish a new Zion and become prosperous. In 1853, the Reorganized Church of Latter Day Saints was founded at a conference held at Zarahemla.

Until 1859, twice-yearly conferences of the reorganized church met here, with representatives coming from southern Wisconsin and northern Illinois. A series of changes in the community gave other communities leadership in the church, and as more "Gentiles" moved into the land, Zarahemla began to lose its purity and holiness. It ceased to exist in 1860. The remaining Blanchardville Branch slowly dissipated as well. The Yellowstone Branch was active for many more years, hence the Saints Road in the countryside of Yellowstone Township.

Today, Graceland Cemetery, which contains tombstones of descendents of Joseph Smith, is all that remains. A Wisconsin official historic marker has been approved for the site, but it has not been erected as of the writing of this book.

Located on Highway 78 at County F, Blanchardville, Lafayette County.

In 1844, members of the church of Jesus Christ of Latter Day Saints arrived in the La Crosse area, but they were not the same as those that followed Brigham Young to Utah. Nor were they followers of James Jesse Strang in eastern Wisconsin. Eventually, this sect joined the Reorganized efforts. Lumber from the nearby forests was used to build the Mormon temple in Nauvoo, Illinois. The Mormon Coulee Memorial Park in La Crosse was named after these settlers.

Wisconsin Dells Native American Church

Definitively Christian in theology and dogma, the Native American Church was founded in 1938. Its unique feature is that elders use peyote as a sacramental substance. About 500 attend the Wisconsin Dells church, which was founded in 1961; there are 2 million church members nationwide.

Located between Oak Glen Circle and Arbor Lake East, off Highway 12/16, about 5 miles northwest of Wisconsin Dells, Juneau County, (715) 887-3368.

Unitarian Universalist Sites
First Unitarian Meeting House

The First Unitarian Society of Madison started meeting in 1878 in the State Capitol Building. Nearly 75 years later, the present-day meetinghouse, designed by Frank Lloyd Wright, was erected. Wright's father was a founding member, and Wright, who had been a member since 1938, accepted only a small fee for his work. The world famous building overlooks Lake Mendota and was once a "country church" that is now surrounded by the city of Madison.

The ceiling's curves are meant to suggest the wings of a bird in flight. Although there is no steeple, the building still has impressive height because of the glass prow that is behind the organ in the triangular auditorium. Regular services are held.

First Unitarian Meeting House, Shorewood Hills

Located at 900 University Bay Drive, on the northwest edge of the UW-Madison campus, Shorewood Hills, Dane County, (608) 233-9774.
wrightinwisconsin.org/WisconsinSites/UnitarianMeeting

Labyrinths

The labyrinth is an ancient mystical tool that has recently come back into vogue. It is similar to a maze, except that it has only one narrow path—made up of 11 concentric circles with a 12th in the center. There are 34 turns on the path going into the center, and there is no "wrong" path. Each number of each element in the labyrinth has symbolic religious significance. The rose shape in the center is universally recognized as a symbol for enlightenment.

Labyrinths can be portable or permanent, made of grass or carpet or stone. The walker enters into a meditative state while walking along the winding path (about a third of a mile long).

These are some of the labyrinths in Wisconsin:

Madison Christian Community (Stillpoint). Outdoor grass (open all the time) and indoor carpet (call for schedule). 7118 Old Sauk Road, Madison, (608) 836-1455.

Sinsinawa Mound. Canvas and an outdoor permanent rock labyrinth. See listing for Sinsinawa Mound Convent and Retreat Center on page 157. Always open to the public. (608) 748-4411.

Cedar Valley Retreat Center. Outdoor grass. 5349 Highway D, near West Bend, (262) 629-5435.

Siena Center. Both indoor and outdoor (grass) labyrinths. 5635 Erie Street, Wind Point (north of Racine), (262) 639-4100.

Calvary Presbyterian Church. Indoor. 935 W. Wisconsin Avenue, Milwaukee, (414) 271-8782.

St. Ann's Church (nondenominational). Indoor and portable. 5933 W. National Avenue, West Allis, (414) 259-1229.

First Congregational United Church of Christ (Stillpoint). Indoor. 1609 University Avenue, Madison, (608) 233-9751.

Labyrinth locator Web site: gracecathedral.org/labyrinth/locator/index.shtml

Stone labyrinth at Sinsinawa Conference and Retreat Center

Unity Chapel

Frank Lloyd Wright contributed to the building of this chapel in his youth; the building was designed by the Lloyd Jones family and built in 1886. The historic landmark includes a chapel graveyard with a gravestone (cenotaph) for Frank Lloyd Wright and his family. His body was actually reburied at Taliesin West in Arizona, but his gravestone still exists here. First Unitarian Universalist Society (Madison) sponsors summer services. It is available for weddings and memorials. The site is on the National Register of Historic Places.

Located on County T (Rainbow Road) at Highway 23, about 3 miles south of Spring Green, Iowa County, (608) 233-3776 or (608) 233-9774. unitychapel.org

Free Congregation Hall

The Free Congregation of Sauk County, a Unitarian fellowship, was part of the once-prominent free-thought movement.

The lay-led congregation (Free Congregation Unitarian Fellowship) was established in 1854 as a German Humanism group (also known as Freie Germeinde). Known as Freethinkers Hall, the large building was erected in 1884 and is on the National Register of Historic Places. The building is still in use.

The congregation's purpose was to "unite the foes of clericalism, official dishonesty, and hypocrisy, and to unite the friends of truth of uprightness and honesty." The congregation aligned with the Unitarians in 1955.

Located at 309 Polk Street, Sauk City, Sauk County, (608) 643-3131.

*B*uddhist Sites

Madison Zen Center

The oldest Zen Center building in Wisconsin, the Madison Zen Center is affiliated with the Zen Center of Rochester, New York, under Sensei Bodhin Kjolhede. Many members travel regularly between the two. There is a regular sitting schedule, and an introduction to Buddhist practice is held the first Monday of each month.

Located at 1820 Jefferson Street, Madison, Dane County, (608) 255-4488. madisonzen.org

Cambodian Buddhist Society of Wisconsin

This Cambodian temple and grounds serve the 500 Cambodian Buddhists living in the Janesville, Stoughton, and Madison area. Most of the staff speaks Cambodian and little English. A new full temple, 40 feet in height, is in the process of being built over the next three to five years.

Located at 1848 Highway MM, off Highway 14, Oregon, Dane County, (608) 835-8136 or 256-1255.

Stupa shrine at Deer Park Buddhist Center, Oregon

Deer Park Buddhist Center

His Holiness the Dalai Lama has visited the Deer Park Buddhist Center several times, making it his Midwest headquarters. He consecrated a stupa shrine, which is one of a few in the world. Deer Park is a center of Tibetan life in Wisconsin, with monks, nuns, and laypersons living and working together to promote Tibetan Buddhism. The Center sponsors educational and cultural programs and interfaith dialogue. Weekly teachings on the graduated path to enlightenment are offered, and a Sunday morning service by teacher Geshe Sopa is held weekly. Visitors are asked to call ahead because the schedule changes.

Located at 4548 Schneider Road, off Highway 14, Oregon, Dane County, (608) 835-5572. deerparkcenter.org

Mahayana Dharma Center

Monks from the Namgyal Monastery (Gelug order) construct a Tibetan sand mandala each summer. At this Buddhist center, Tibetan medicine classes and related subjects are offered. They are working to open the first Tibetan medical center in North America. Global View, next door, features south Asian art, artifacts and textiles. Founded in 1979, the Center is open to all.

Located at 6593 Clyde Road, 8 miles southwest of Spring Green, Dane County, (608) 583-5311. dharmacenter.globalview-intl.com

Jewish Sites

Congregation Sons of Abraham

An egalitarian synagogue affiliated with the United Synagogue of Conservative Judaism, this was built in 1948. The synagogue serves a radius of more than 40 miles. In the vestibule, beautifully carved into the stone is a line from the Book of Isaiah: "My house shall be called a house of prayer for all peoples."

Located at 1820 Main Street, La Crosse, La Crosse County, (608) 784-7648. uscj.org/central/lacrosse

Inscription in the vestibule of the Congregation Sons of Abraham, La Crosse

Gates of Heaven Synagogue

The oldest surviving synagogue in the Midwest and the third oldest in the nation, Gates of Heaven Synagogue was built in 1863 and originally stood near the square on West Washington Street in downtown Madison. It was moved to James Madison Park in the 1970s. No longer used as a synagogue, it was purchased by the city of Madison and is used for a variety of purposes, including weddings.

Located at James Madison Park, 300 E. Gorham Street (corner of North Butler), Madison, Dane County. For information, contact the Madison City Parks Department. (608) 266-4711.

Other Sites

Wisconsin Dells

Natives believe the Great Spirit in the form of a snake created the Dells. The area has many auspicious stone formations and some of the most beautiful scenery in the United States.

The area has been heavily populated and influenced by Native Americans. Though much of this influence has been secularized for material consumption, the area is still considered legitimately sacred to many. "An Expression of Life," Native American ceremonial dancing, is held evenings in the summer months. It is the only such performance in upper Midwest. Information is available by calling (608) 253-9994.

Located on Highway 16, northwest of the city of Wisconsin Dells, Sauk County.

Spirit Oak

The "Spirit Oak" was a well-known presence on the fourth fairway at the Blackhawk Country Club, blocking the view of the hole from the tee. At 227 years old, the large tree was considered a permanent landmark. But the bur oak fell during a storm in 1974. Cross-sections are in the lounge at the country club. In *Autobiography of the Spirit Oak*, L. J. Markwardt wrote a life story of the tree. Access is limited, so call the country club before visiting.

Located on the grounds of the Blackhawk Country Club, Shorewood Hills, Dane County, (608) 231-2454.

Parfrey's Glen State Natural Area

Glen is a Scottish word for a narrow rocky ravine, and in Wisconsin there are some beautiful glens. Perhaps the most inspiring is Parfrey's Glen. Named after the Englishman who acquired the land in 1865, it became a tourist attraction. In 1882, there was talk of a hotel being built at the site. The glen was selected

Parfrey's Glen,
near Devil's Lake
State Park

as the first State Natural Area in 1950 and is protected along with many species of rare vegetation—some that grow only in the glen. Reaching a depth of nearly 100 feet in the sandstone conglomerate, it has a mountain-type stream flowing through it.

Located 4 miles south of Devil's Lake State Park on County DL.
Take Highway 113 south from Baraboo to County DL and turn left.
The entrance is a few miles on the left.

Ferry Bluff State Natural Area

Ferry Bluff, State Natural Area number 217, rises more than 300 feet above the Wisconsin River. It is the wintering site for eagles and the home to other endangered birds of prey. The steep climb can be ambitious for nonhikers. At the top is one of the most spectacular natural views in the state.

Located southwest of Sauk City, Sauk County. From Highway 60/12 west of Sauk City,
take Highway 60 west 4 miles to Ferry Bluff Road. Go south on it just over a mile to the end
where signs and maps will guide you. State Natural Areas Program, (608) 266-0394.

Governor Dodge State Park

Historic sites at this state park include an old Norwegian cemetery dating back to 1861 and a 30-foot waterfall. Deer Cove Rock Shelter, a 35-foot rock overhang, served as shelter for primitive peoples. The park is in the Driftless

Region, an area not touched by the glaciers but encircled by them. The sandstone bluffs date back 450 million years to when seas covered the area.

Located at 4175 Highway 23, north of Dodgeville, Iowa County, (608) 935-2315.

Circle Sanctuary

Circle Sanctuary is home to the International Nature Spirituality Center and the first federally recognized Wiccan Church in the United States, founded in 1974. The oft-misunderstood belief system is a form of nature spirituality. Wiccans believe in a feminine divinity, along with a variety of other gods and goddesses. Circle Sanctuary provides a place for pagans of all types to practice their earth-based religious beliefs—Wiccan ways, Shamanism, Goddess studies, Celtic spirituality, etc.

Spirit Rock at Circle Sanctuary, near Barneveld

Circle Sanctuary is 200-acre nature preserve with almost 60 species of birds, as well as meditation trails and various ceremonial sites. The beautiful Spirit Rock, a large natural rock formation, provides a splendid overview of the area. The Stone Circle is made of natural stones and various trinkets from all over the world. There are a wide variety of shrines—for dogs, cats, birds, deer, frogs—and many have buried beloved pets at the shrines.

The facility is open by appointment or on Wiccan holy days. Visits are free but must be planned in advance. Some events have admission costs. Donations are accepted.

Located on County K between Highway 18/151 and Highway 14,
near Barneveld, Dane County, (608) 924-2216. circlesanctuary.org/

Pachamama

This nonprofit organization offers Shamanic training, drumming circles, and men's and women's gatherings. The facility is operated by Jaes Seis, a teacher and practitioner of Shamanism with more than 20 years of experience. The 120-acre spiritual gathering place is located in the beautiful Driftless Region. "Our vision is to heal and be healed by the land and each other, to awaken and be awakened by the Spirits of the land."

Located near Richland Center, Richland County, (608) 647-6036.

Dane County Hospital and Home Memorial

This poignant memorial monument was dedicated in 1993 for a graveyard of almost 500, but the small white headstones mysteriously vanished. It says, "On these beautiful grounds lie the remains of the mentally impaired and poor who spend their last earthly days here."

Located at Badger Prairie Health Care Center,
on old Highway 18/151, Verona, Dane County.

Paul and Matilda Wegner Grotto

Paul and Matilda Wegner created this grotto between 1929 and 1942, including religious, secular, and fraternal symbolism and some fun and fanciful constructions. Its creators were self-taught artists from Germany. An interesting feature is the "Glass Church" chapel with the "One God One Brotherhood" banner. The grotto is reminiscent of the one in Dickeyville, but it is not overtly Catholic. The site is open for self-guided tours daily from late spring to late fall.

Located on Daylight Road and Highway 71, 1.5 miles south of Cataract,
Monroe County, (608) 269-8680. netcolony.com/pets/agilitynut/wegnergrotto.html;
interestingideas.com/roadside/wisc/weg/weg2.htm

*I*n this world abode of ours,
May communication drive away miscommunication,
May peace drive away anarchy,
May generosity drive away selfishness,
May benevolence drive away hostility
May compassionate words prevail over false protestations,
May truth prevail over falsehood.

—From a Dahm Afrigan prayer

Fraternal Orders and Sacred Places

Throughout Wisconsin (and the United States) are buildings where fraternal and civic groups meet. Some of the most impressive are Temples of Freemasonry. Other fraternal groups include Knights of Pythias, Knights of Columbus, and the Odd Fellows; civic groups include the Elks, Eagles, and Moose.

Freemasonry is the oldest, largest and most distinguished of these. It is also the most maligned. The Freemasons tend toward social atmospheres and exist to improve the individual, neighborhoods, towns, and cities. One of the requirements for Freemasonry is that the individual believes in God, but Freemasonry does not promote a specific theology. The "lodges" often have moral lessons or ideals to follow. Members are often strong and avid supporters of churches and other religious organizations, because a fraternal or civic group is not, in and of its own, religious.

So, is a building dedicated to these endeavors "sacred"? Perhaps. Perhaps not. However, there are a few sites that are worth mentioning:

The Tripoli Shrine Temple Mosque (See listing in chapter 1.)

Wisconsin Odd Fellows of Mineral Point built the first **Odd Fellows** lodge hall (1838) west of the Allegheny Mountains. It is now a fascinating museum that houses Odd Fellows artifacts. Open daily June 1 through September 1, 9 a.m. to 3 p.m.

Located at 1121/2 Front Street (at State Street), Mineral Point,
Iowa County, (608) 987-3093.

The Masonic Cemetery is just down the hill from Olive Branch Lodge 6 in New Diggings. This is the only consecrated Masonic cemetery and the oldest Masonic cemetery in Wisconsin, making it one of the oldest in the country. It is still in use but under the administration of Benton Lodge No. 268.

Located on County W, New Diggings, Lafayette County, (608) 965-3575.

•

Lists of Sites by Religious Category

THESE LISTS ARE INTENDED as organizational tools and guides to the sites in the book. Due to space limitations, they do not include all the state's sacred sites. In addition, there may have been problems adequately identifying a site of historic significance due to inaccurate or conflicting source materials.

1. Baptist Sites
Greater Milwaukee
1859	Freewill Baptist Church, New Berlin

Southeast
1845	First Baptist Church of Merton, Merton
1857	St. Paul Missionary Baptist Church, Racine
1872	First Baptist Church, Waukesha
1968	Maranatha Baptist Bible College, Watertown

Northeast
1834	Brothertown Baptists, Brothertown
1859	New Denmark Baptists, New Denmark
1944	Green Lake Conference Center, Green Lake

Southwest
1846	Seventh-Day Baptist Church, Albion
1854	Albion Academy (now a museum), Albion

2. Buddhist Temples
Greater Milwaukee
1977	Milwaukee Shambhala Center, Milwaukee (north)
1979	Milwaukee Zen Center, Milwaukee (north)
1981	Milwaukee Mindfulness Practice Center, Milwaukee (east)
1996	Phuoc-Hou Buddhist Temple of Milwaukee, Milwaukee (west)
1999	Wat Pathonmaphoutharan (Lao), Milwaukee (west)

Southeast
1987	Original Root Zen Center, Racine

Southwest
1974	Madison Zen Center, Madison
1979	Mahayana Dharma Center, Spring Green
1979	Deer Park Buddhist Center, Oregon (Dane County)
1996	Cambodian Buddhist Society of Wisconsin, Oregon (Dane County)

3. Catholic Sites
Greater Milwaukee
1400	St. Joan of Arc Chapel, Milwaukee (downtown)
1674	Pere Marquette Park, Milwaukee (downtown)
1846	Old St. Mary Church, Milwaukee (downtown)

1847	Cathedral of St. John the Evangelist, Milwaukee (downtown)
1847	St. Stephen Catholic Church, Milwaukee (south)
1849	Holy Trinity Roman Catholic Church, Milwaukee (downtown)
1866	Marian Center/St. Francis Seminary Complex, St. Francis
1881	Marquette University, Milwaukee (downtown)
1893	Gesu Parish Church, Milwaukee (downtown)
1893	St. Patrick's Roman Catholic Church, Milwaukee (south)
1896	Basilica of St. Josaphat, Milwaukee (south)
1917	St. George Melkite Greek Catholic Church, Milwaukee (downtown)
1923	St. Benedict the Moor Catholic Church, Milwaukee (downtown)
1929	Sacred Heart School of Theology and Shrine, Hales Corners
1968	Archbishop Cousins Archdiocesan Retreat Center, St. Francis
1980	Archdiocesan Marian Shrine, Milwaukee (west)

Southeast

1843	St. Henry Parish, Watertown
1845	Holy Cross Church, Holy Cross
1858	Holy Hill National Shrine of Mary, Hubertus
1858	St. John the Baptist Church, Jefferson
1859	St. Lawrence Church, Jefferson
1863	St. Wenceslaus Church—The Island Church, Waterloo
1876	Nativity of Mary Parish (St. Mary's), Janesville
1882	St. Mary's Roman Catholic Church, Port Washington
1882	St. Mary of the Lake Church, Lake Church
1929	St. Francis Retreat Center, Burlington
1945	St. Benedict Abbey, Benet Lake
1960	Siena Center, Racine
1964	Schoenstatt Center, Delafield

Northeast

1669	Mission of St. Francis Xavier, Oconto
1822	Allouez Catholic Cemetery and Chapel, Allouez
1847	St. Martin's Church, Ashford
1852	St. Catherine's Church, Calumet County
1854	St. Gregory's Church, St. Nazianz
1856	St. John Baptist Church, Montello
1857	St. John the Baptist Church, Johnsburg
1857	St. Lawrence Seminary, Mount Calvary
1861	Chapel of Our Lady of Good Help, New Franken
1862	St. John the Baptist Catholic Church, St. John
1865	St. Mary's Convent, St. Nazianz
1876	Old St. Joseph's Church, De Pere
1878	Church of the Atonement, Door County
1883	St Mary's Church, Menasha
1886	Church of the Assumption of the Blessed Virgin Mary, Pulaski
1892	St. Lawrence Catholic Church, Stangleville
1898	St. Francis Xavier Cathedral, Green Bay
1899	St. Norbert Abbey Ministry and Life Center, De Pere
1901	Julieski Millennium Shrine, Pulaski
1905	St. Claudius Church, St. Cloud
1915	St. Peter's Church, Fond du Lac County
1934	Monte Alverno Retreat Center, Appleton
1935	St. Francis Xavier Grotto, Brussels
1936	St. Mary's Springs, Fond du Lac
1951	Holy Name Retreat House, Chambers Island
?	St. Joseph's Retreat Center, Baileys Harbor
?	St. John the Baptist Church, Egg Harbor

Northwest

1665	La Pointe du Saint Espirit, Madeline Island
1870	Our Lady of the Falls, Lourdes Grotto, Chippewa Falls
1874	St. Clare Center for Spirituality, Custer
1881	Flambeau Mission Church, Rusk County
1884	St. Joseph's Church, Stevens Point
1888	St. Ann's Church and Cemetery, Rib Lake
1891	Holy Family Catholic Church, Bayfield
1896	St. Joseph's Chapel, Eau Claire
1927	Cathedral of Christ the King, Superior
1927	Rudolph Grotto Gardens and Wonder Cave, Chippewa County
1929	Sacred Heart of Jesus Church, Eau Claire
1964	St. Bede Retreat and Conference Center, Eau Claire

Southwest

1836	St. Gabriel Catholic Church, Prairie du Chien
1838	Congregation of St. Paul's, Mineral Point
1838	St. Thomas Parish, Potosi
1841	St. Matthew's Catholic Church, Shullsburg
1844	St. Augustine's Church, New Diggings
1844	Sinsinawa Mound Convent, Sinsinawa
1846	St. Andrew Parish, Tennyson
1846	SS Anthony and Phillip Parish, Highland
1847	St. Patrick's Catholic Church, Benton
1848	St. Norbert House, Roxbury
1854	Cathedral of St. Raphael, Madison
1856	St. Mary's Ridge Church, Cashton
1857	St. Mary of the Oaks Chapel, Dane County
1861	Holy Redeemer Mission Church, Dane County
1862	Durward's Glen, Columbia County
1862	St. Barnabas Church, Mazomanie
1866	St. John the Evangelist Church, Spring Green
1880	Our Lady of Sorrows Chapel, La Crosse
1885	St. Patrick's Parish, Lodi
1903	Our Lady of the Fields Shrine, Sauk County
1928	The Plain Shrine at St. Anne's Hill, Plain
1930	Dickeyville Grotto, Dickeyville
1930	Holy Family Grotto, St. Joseph
1930	Solitude Ridge Hermitages, St. Joseph
1940	Maria Angelorum Chapel, La Crosse
1948	Schoenstatt Shrine, Madison
1949	Queen of the Holy Rosary Mediatrix Peace Shrine, Necedah (Old Catholic)
1953	St. Benedict Center Monastery, Middleton
1958	Camp Gray, Lake Delton
1960	Cathedral of St. Joseph the Workman, La Crosse
2001	Our Lady of Guadalupe National Shrine, La Crosse County

4. Effigy Mounds

Almost 3,000 years ago, Native Americans began building mounds of earth throughout the green woodlands of the region that is now Wisconsin. They continued until about 1200 C.E. The State Historical Society of Wisconsin has recorded more than 14,000 mounds in the state—more than anywhere else in the world. The largest percentage of these mounds is in the southwest part of the state, especially in the Madison area. Native Americans, as well as people of other heritages, honor these mounds as sacred.

Usually built around lakes and rivers, the mounds are deeply mysterious to those who visit them today. Part of the mystery is that no one knows exactly what the builders intended. Some mounds are in the shape of animals (eagles, rabbits, bears); others are conical or oval shaped. Some are burial mounds, while others contain nothing but dirt. Some people believe they relate to star constellations. Strangely, their shapes are best viewed from the air—the one vantage point that would have been impossible for their builders to utilize.

To visit a mound is to take a step back to the time when ancient peoples lived off the land in a way we cannot comprehend. For them, the spirit world and the material world were not separate, in the way that it seems for most of us. For them, the very earth was alive. To be properly reverent, one approaches a mound in silence and sprinkles tobacco while addressing the Great Spirit. Under the Burial Sites Preservation Law, prehistoric burial mounds are to be afforded the same treatment as cemetery plots.

The area near Madison's four lakes (Monona, Mendota, Waubesa, and Kegonsa, all in Dane County) is home to more than 1,500 remaining mounds. Many more were destroyed due to urban development. The lakes themselves were considered sacred, as was the land around them (especially the isthmus between Mendota and Monona). Some of the largest mounds in the world are located on the grounds of what is now the Mendota Mental Health Institute. A bird-shaped mound there had an original wingspan of more than 624 feet—wider than two football fields. The area also has some unusually shaped mounds: one a panther with a curved tail and another a deer with four legs (instead of two, which was more common).

The late Charles E. Brown, an archeologist and State Historical Society museum director, led the earliest efforts to protect the mounds from destruction. He located mounds or mound groups on the University of Wisconsin–Madison campus, in Burrows Park, at Maple Bluff, Bernards Park, the Mendota Mental Health Institute and the State Memorial Hospital grounds, Morris Park, Fox Bluff, Kennedy Pond, West Point, Camp Sunrise, Mendota Beach, Merrill Springs, Blackhawk Country Club, Eagle Heights, and on Picnic Point.

Nearby Jefferson County also offers many mounds along sacred Lake Koshkonong. A group of 11 mounds, closely aligned, is located on Old Highway 26. These are part of the General Atkinson Group, which originally contained 72 mounds within a one-mile area. The mounds can be seen on a quick walking tour, which includes markers and an old "Indian trail." Just west of Fort Atkinson, you'll find the only complete "intaglio" in existence. It's a "negative" mound, a symmetrical hole in the ground. Like the other mounds, its existence is a mystery.

Most of the mounds are open to the public. You'll have to pay a fee if you visit mounds in a state park. When visiting mounds, it's okay to take pictures—but please be quiet and respectful (even if there's no one else around).

LOCATION	SITE	TYPE						
		Bird	Water	Bear	Deer	Linear	Conical	Other
Greater Milwaukee								
Milwaukee	Lake Park Mound							x
Southeast								
Fort Atkinson	Panther Intaglio		x					
Lake Mills	Aztalan Village State Park						x	x
Koshkonong	Jefferson County Indian Mounds		x				x	x
Beloit	Beloit College Effigy Mounds		x	x		x	x	
Whitewater	Whitewater Effigy Mound Park	x	x	x	x		x	
West Bend	Lizard Mound County Park	x	x	x		x	x	x
Silver Lake	Turtle Mound		x					
Waukesha	Cutler Mound Group						x	
Northeast								
Stockbridge	Calumet County Park		x			x	x	
Shorewood	High Cliff Mounds		x			x	x	x
Sheboygan	Sheboygan Indian Mound Park	x	x		x	x	x	x
Waupaca	Taylor Lake Mound		x					
Hancock	Whistler Mound Group						x	x
Menasha	Smith Park Mound Group	x					x	x

LOCATION — SITE — TYPE

LOCATION	SITE	Bird	Water	Bear	Deer	Linear	Conical	Other
Northwest								
Rice Lake	Rice Lake Indian Mounds							x
Menomonie	Wakanda Park Mounds						x	
Lake Tomahawk	Indian Mounds Campground						x	
Trempealeau	Trempealeau Mounds						x	x
Southwest								
Madison	Burrows Park Bird Effigy Mound	x						
Madison	Edgewood College Mound Group	x						x
Madison	Edna Taylor Conservancy Mounds	x					x	
Madison	Elmside Park Mounds	x						
Madison	Farwell's Point Mound Group	x	x			x		
Madison	Forest Hill Cemetery Mound Group	x	x					
Madison	Gallistel Woods Mound Group	x				x	x	x
Madison	Hudson Park Effigy Mound			x				
Madison	Mendota State Hospital Mound Group	x	x	x	x	x	x	x
Madison	Observatory Hill Mounds		x	x			x	x
Madison	Picnic Point Mound Group							x
Madison	Spring Harbor Mound Group				x			
Madison	Vilas Circle Bear Effigy	x						
Madison	Vilas Park Effigy Mounds	x	x					x
McFarland	Lewis Mound Group			x		x	x	x
Middleton	Morris Mound Group	x				x		
Monona	Outlet Mound							x
Shorewood	Blackhawk C. C. Mound Group	x		x			x	
Necedah	Cranberry Creek	x	x			x	x	x
Baraboo	Devil's Lake Bird Effigy Mound	x						
Baraboo	Devil's Lake Mound Group			x	x		x	x
Baraboo	Terminal Moraine Mound Group		x			x	x	
New Lisbon	Indian Mounds Park	x	x	x		x	x	
Fairfield	Man Mound Park							x
Wisconsin Dells	Kingsley Bend Indian Mounds		x		x			x
Avoca	Avoca Mound Group				x	x		
Bridgeport	Wayside Mounds					x	x	
Eagle Corners	Bird Effigy Mound	x						
Wyalusing	Wyalusing State Park Mound Groups	x	x	x		x	x	
La Crosse	Myrick Park Effigy Mound			x				x
Cassville	Nelson Dewey Group						x	x
Marquette, Iowa	Effigy Mound National Monument	x		x		x	x	x

5. Episcopal Sites

Greater Milwaukee

1836	St Paul's Episcopal Church, Milwaukee (downtown)
1850	Forest Home Cemetery and Chapel, Milwaukee (west)
1851	St. James Episcopal Church, Milwaukee (downtown)
1866	All Saints' Episcopal Cathedral, Milwaukee (downtown)

Southeast

1836	Carriage House Chapel, Dousman
1839	St. Matthew's Episcopal Church, Kenosha
1841	St. John in the Wilderness Episcopal Church, Elkhorn
1841	St. Luke's Episcopal Church, Whitewater
1841	St. Paul's Episcopal Church, Beloit
1842	Nashotah House Seminary Grounds, Delafield
1842	St. Alban's Episcopal Church, Sussex

1842	St. Luke's Episcopal Church, Racine
1844	Christ Episcopal Church, Delavan
1844	St. Mathias Episcopal Church, Waukesha
1847	St. Paul's Church, Watertown
1852	St. John Chrysostom Church, Delafield
1852	DeKoven Center, Racine
1871	Holy Trinity Episcopal Church, Waupun
1878	St. Mary's Episcopal Church, Dousman

Northeast

1826	Christ Church, Green Bay
1836	Holy Apostles Church, Oneida
1847	Our Lady of Walsingham Shrine at Grace Church, Sheboygan
1860	St. Peter's Episcopal Church, Ripon
1875	Cathedral Church of St. Paul, Fond du Lac
1878	St. Agnes Church, Algoma
1887	Trinity Episcopal Church, Oshkosh
1899	Convent of the Holy Nativity, Fond du Lac
?	Camp Webb, Wautoma

Northwest

1870	Christ Episcopal Church, Bayfield
1909	Christ Church Cathedral, Eau Claire

Southwest

1836	Holy Trinity Church, Prairie du Chien
1845	Trinity Church, Mineral Point
1846	Grace Episcopal Church, Madison
1853	St. John the Baptist Church, Portage
1898	Christ Church of La Crosse, La Crosse

6. Islamic Sites

Greater Milwaukee

1930	Muhammad Mosque # 3, Milwaukee
1974	Masjid Sultan Muhammad, Milwaukee
1976	Masjid al Imam—Islamic Society of Milwaukee, Milwaukee
1999	Ahmadiyya Movement in Islam Center, Milwaukee

Southeast

1966	Masjid Tawheed, Kenosha

Northwest

1997	Masjid of Northern Wisconsin, Altoona

Southwest

1960	Islamic Center of Madison, Madison
1995	Masjid us Sunnah, Madison

7. Jewish Sites

Greater Milwaukee

1856	Eman-El B'Ne Jeshurun Congregation, Milwaukee
1884	Congregation Beth Israel, Glendale
1925	Congregation Beth Israel Synagogue, Milwaukee
1951	Congregation Shalom, Fox Point

Southeast

1902	Congregation Aguda Achim Chabad, Mequon
1951	Olin-Sang-Ruby Union Institute (OSRUI), Oconomowoc

Northeast

1883	Temple Zion (Moses Montifort) Synagogue (inactive), Appleton
1899	Beth El Congregation, Sheboygan
1949	Congregation B'nai Israel, Oshkosh

1954   Anshe Poale Zedek Synagogue, Manitowoc
?   Sheboygan Hebrew Cemetery, Kohler
Southwest
1863   Gates of Heaven Synagogue (inactive), Madison
1948   Congregation Sons of Abraham, La Crosse

8. Lutheran Sites
Greater Milwaukee
1878   Trinity Evangelical Lutheran Church, Milwaukee (downtown)
Southeast
1843   Norway Evangelical Lutheran Church, Waterford
1844   Jefferson Prairie Church, Clinton
1844   Holy Trinity Lutheran Church, Theinsville
1845   David Star Church, Washington County
1855   Heart Prairie Lutheran Church, Whitewater
1863   Wisconsin Lutheran Seminary, Mequon
1871   Bethany Lutheran Church, Brodhead
1881   Concordia University, Mequon
1899   St. Paul's Lutheran Church, Janesville
1944   Lutherdale Bible Camp, Elkhorn
Northeast
1845   Faith Lutheran Church, Valders
1882   Free Evangelical Lutheran Church, Ephraim
1901   Lutheran Indian Mission, Shawano County
1902   Zion Lutheran Church, Appleton
1939   Bjorklunden Chapel, Baileys Harbor
1945   St. Paul's Evangelical Lutheran Church, Tipler
Northwest
1873   Sabylund Lutheran Church, Lund
Southwest
1844   First Koshkonong Lutheran Church, Dane County
1844   East Wiota Lutheran Church, Wiota
1844   West Koshkonong Lutheran Church, Dane County
1845   Springdale Lutheran Church, Springdale
1852   Hauge Log Church, Daleyville
1853   Coon Valley Lutherans, Coon Valley
1854   Perry Lutheran Church, Daleyville
1856   Halfway Creek Lutheran Church, Holmen
1856   Vermont Lutheran Church, Dane County
1861   York Memorial Church and Old York Church, Blanchardville
1868   Yellowstone Lutheran Church, Lafayette County

9. Methodist Sites
Northeast
1832   Smithfield Church Site, Kimberly
1848   Camp Byron, Brownsville
1851   Rock Hill Chapel and Cemetery, Dalton
1858   Greenville Church, Greenville
1890   Algoma Boulevard Methodist Church, Oshkosh
1919   Lawrence Memorial Chapel, Appleton
1945   Lucerne Camp and Retreat Center, Neshkoro
Southwest
1830   Roundtree-Mitchell Cottage, Platteville
1850   Rutland Church, Rutland
1851   Linden Methodist Church, Linden
1851   Willerup United Methodist Church, Cambridge

1851 Wyoming Methodist Church, Wyoming
1853 First Methodist Episcopal Church, Baraboo
1859 Welsh Calvinistic Methodist Church, Bangor
1861 Primitive Methodist Church, Jenkynsville
1862 Hyde Chapel (Union Congregational Church), Ridgeway
1882 Pleasant Ridge Cemetery, Beetown

10. Eastern Orthodox Sites

Greater Milwaukee
1912 St. Sava Serbian Orthodox Cathedral, Milwaukee (south)
1927 SS Cyril and Methodius Church OCA, Milwaukee (south)
1961 Holy Resurrection Armenian Apostolic, Milwaukee (south)
1961 Annunciation Greek Orthodox Church, Wauwatosa
1985 St. John the Baptist Armenian Church, Greenfield

Southeast
1912 St. Nicholas Church OCA, Kenosha
1925 St. Mesrob Armenian Apostolic Church, Racine
1994 Zion Orthodox Hermitage (ROCOR), Richwood
? St. Mary and St. Antonios Coptic Church, Waterford

Northeast
1910 St. Spyridon Greek Orthodox Church, Sheboygan

Northwest
1902 Holy Trinity Church OCA, Clayton
1906 St. Mary Church OCA, Cornucopia
1906 St. John the Baptist Church OCA, Stanley
1908 Holy Assumption Church OCA, Lublin

Southwest
1912 St. Elias Antiochian Church, La Crosse
1956 Assumption Greek Orthodox Church, Madison
1986 St. Isaac of Syria Russian Orthodox Skete, Boscobel

11. Presbyterian Sites

Greater Milwaukee
1870 Calvary Presbyterian Church, Milwaukee (downtown)
1873 Immanuel Presbyterian Church, Milwaukee (downtown)

Southeast
1842 Jerusalem Welsh Presbyterian Church, Wales
1851 First Presbyterian Church, Racine
1857 Bethesda Chapel, Waukesha
1860 First Presbyterian Church of Ottawa, Ottawa
1873 Zion Welsh Presbyterian, Pewaukee
1873 Salem Presbyterian Cemetery, Wales

Northeast
1893 First Presbyterian Church, Oshkosh

Southwest
1847 Carmel Presbyterian Church, Rewey
1849 Oakland Cambridge Presbyterian Church, Cambridge

12. Retreat Centers by County

The retreat centers listed here may have requirements and/or limitations about the use of their facilities. Some will only accommodate activities related to their religious or spiritual tradition. Others are open to anyone but have restrictions. Some consider themselves open to the public. Note that some centers listed here do not appear in the main section of the book.

Brown (Northeast)
De Pere St. Norbert Abbey Ministry and Life Center

Denmark	Bridge Between Ecumenical Retreat Center
Clark (Northwest)	
Willard	Christine Center
Columbia (Southwest)	
Baraboo	Durward's Glen
Crawford (Southwest)	
Ferryville	Sugar Creek Bible Camp
Dane (Southwest)	
Barneveld	Circle Sanctuary
Middleton	St. Benedict Center
Monona	San Damiano Center
Oregon	Deer Park Buddhist Center
Dodge (Southeast)	
Richwood	Zion Orthodox Hermitage
Door (Northeast)	
Baileys Harbor	St. Joseph's Retreat Center
Chambers Island	Holy Name Retreat House
Ellison Bay	The Clearing
Eau Claire (Northwest)	
Eau Claire	St. Bede Retreat and Conference Center
Fond du Lac (Northeast)	
Brownsville	Byron Center
Fond du Lac	Convent of the Holy Nativity
Grant (Southwest)	
Sinsinawa	Sinsinawa Mound Convent and Retreat Center
Green Lake (Northeast)	
Green Lake	Green Lake Conference Center
Jefferson (Southeast)	
Lake Mills	Namaste Center of Wisconsin
Juneau (Southwest)	
Wonewoc	Western Wisconsin Spiritual Center
Kenosha (Southeast)	
Benet Lake	St. Benedict Abbey
La Crosse (Southwest)	
La Crosse	Franciscan Spirituality Center
St. Joseph	Solitude Ridge Hermitages
Manitowoc (Northeast)	
Kiel	Pathways of Light
Marathon (Northwest)	
Marathon	St. Anthony Retreat Center
Marquette (Northeast)	
Montello	Camp Corbin
Neshkoro	Lucerne Camp and Retreat Center
Westfield	Pine Lake United Methodist Camp
Milwaukee (Milwaukee)	
St. Francis	Archbishop Cousins Archdiocesan Retreat Center
Monroe (Southwest)	
Cashton	Convent House
Outagamie (Northeast)	
Appleton	Monte Alverno Retreat Center
Portage (Northwest)	
Polonia	St. Clare Center for Spirituality
Racine (Southeast)	
Burlington	St. Francis Retreat Center
Racine	DeKoven Center
Racine	Original Root Zen Center

Racine	Siena Center
Richland (Southwest)	
Boscobel	St. Isaac of Syria Russian Orthodox Skete
Excelsior	Excelsior Retreat Center
Richland Center	Camp Woodbrooke (Quaker)
Sauk (Southwest)	
Lake Delton	Camp Gray
Sawyer (Northwest)	
Ladysmith	Servite Center for Life
Trego	Marvin Schwan Retreat and Conference Center
Trempealeau (Northwest)	
Galesville	Marynook Retreat and Conference Center
Osseo	The Woodlands
Vilas (Northwest)	
St. Germaine	Moon Beach Camp UCC
Walworth (Southeast)	
Elkhorn	Lutherdale
Elkhorn	St. Vincent Pallotti Center
Lake Geneva	Covenant Harbor (Geneva Bay Centre)
Walworth	Inspiration Center
Washington (Southeast)	
Hubertus	Holy Hill National Shrine of Mary
West Bend	Aldin Acres Retreat Center
West Bend	Cedar Valley Retreat Center
Waukesha (Southeast)	
Delafield	Schoenstatt Center
Oconomowoc	Olin-Sang-Ruby Union Institute
Oconomowoc	Redemptorist Retreat Center
Oconomowoc	Our Mother of Perpetual Help Retreat Center
Delafield	Nashotah House Seminary Grounds
Waushara (Northeast)	
Mt. Morris	Mt. Morris Camp and Conference Center
Wautoma	Camp Webb
Winnebago (Northeast)	
Menasha	Mount Tabor Center
Oshkosh	Jesuit Retreat House

13. Unitarian Universalist Sites

Greater Milwaukee

1892	First Unitarian Society of Milwaukee, Milwaukee

Southeast

1842	Olympia Brown Unitarian Universalist Church, Racine
1878	United Unitarian and Universalist Church, Mukwonago
?	Bradford Community Church Unitarian Universalist, Kenosha

Northwest

1914	First Universalist Church, Wausau

Southwest

1858	Stoughton Universalist Church (inactive but open as museum), Stoughton
1860	Universalist Church (inactive but open as arts center), Monroe
1884	Free Congregation Hall, Sauk City
1886	Unity Chapel, Spring Green
1951	First Unitarian Meeting House, Shorewood Hills

14. United Church of Christ (Congregationalist) Sites

Southeast

1840	St. Paul's Evangelical Church, Colgate
1845	First Congregational Church, Janesville
1850	Shopiere Congregational Church, Shopiere
1857	Fulton Congregational Church, Fulton
1867	First Congregational Church, Waukesha
1868	St. John's UCC, Germantown
?	First Congregational Church, Kenosha

Northeast

1863	First Congregational Church, Ripon
1891	Christian Endeavor Academy, Endeavor

Northwest

1833	Mission House, Madeline Island
1856	Home Mission, Wisconsin Rapids
1878	Winnebago Indian Mission, Black River Falls
?	Moon Beach Camp UCC, St. Germaine

Southwest

1849	Swiss United Church of Christ, New Glarus

General

Selected Bibliography

Benson, John. *Transformative Adventures, Vacations and Retreats: An International Directory.* Portland, Ore: New Millennium Publishing, 1994.

Bowker, John, ed. *The Oxford Dictionary of World Religions.* New York: Oxford University Press, 1997.

Brockman, Norbert, ed. *Encyclopedia of Sacred Places.* New York: Oxford University Press, 1997.

Devereux, Paul. *Secrets of Ancient and Sacred Sites: The World's Mysterious Heritage.* London: Blandford Press, 1992.

Good, Merle, and Phyllis Pellman Good. *20 Most Asked Questions about the Amish and Mennonites.* Rev. ed. Intercourse, Pa: Good Books, 1995.

Harpur, James. *The Atlas of Sacred Places: Meeting Points of Heaven and Earth.* New York: Henry Holt and Company, 1994.

Hinnels, John R., ed. *A Handbook of Living Religions.* New York: Viking Penguin Inc., 1984.

Hope, Jane. *The Secret Language of the Soul: A Visual Guide to the Spiritual World.* San Francisco: Chronicle Books, 1997.

Lethaby, William. *Architecture, Mysticism and Myth.* 1891. Reprint, New York: George Braziller, Inc., 1974.

Wilson, Colin. *Atlas of Holy Places and Sacred Sites: An Illustrated Guide.* New York: DK Publishing, 1996.

Zirblis, Raymond Paul. *Country Churches.* London: Metro Books, 1998.

North America

Anderson, Arlow W. *The Salt of the Earth: History of Norwegian Danish Methodism in America.* Nashville: Parthenon Press, 1962.

Chester, Laura. *Holy Personal: Looking for Small Private Places of Worship.* Indianapolis: Indiana University Press, 2000.

Chiant, Marilyn J. *America's Religious Architecture: Sacred Places for Every Community.* New York: John Wiley and Sons, 1997.

Coe, Michael, Dean Snow, and Elizabeth Benson. *Atlas of Ancient America.* New York: Facts on File, Inc., 1986.

Directory of the Members of the Conference on the Religious Life in the Americas, 1997.

Guiley, Rosemary Ellen. *Atlas of the Mysterious in North America.* New York: Facts on File, Inc., 1995.

Joy, Janet. *A Place Apart: Houses of Prayer and Retreat Centers in North America.* Self published, 1995.

Kelly, Jack, and Marcia Kelly. *Sanctuaries: A Guide to Lodgings in Monasteries, Abbeys and Retreats in the U.S.* New York: Bell Tower/Harmony Books/Crown Publishers, 1996.

Morreale, Don. *Buddhist America: Centers, Retreats, Practices.* Santa Fe, N. Mex.:John Muir Publications, 1988.

———. *The Complete Guide to Buddhist America.* Boston and London: Shambhala, 1998.

Peterson, Natasha. *Sacred Sites: A Traveler's Guide to North America's Most Powerful, Mystical Landmarks.* Chicago: Contemporary Books, 1988.

Versluis, Arthur. *Sacred Earth: The Spiritual Landscape of Native America.* Rochester, Vt.: Inner Traditions, 1992.

Thornton, Francis Beauchesne. *Catholic Shrines in the United States and Canada.* New York: Wilfred Funk, 1954.

Wisconsin

1999 Wisconsin Bed and Breakfast Directory. Merrill, Wis.: Wisconsin Bed and Breakfast Association, 1999.

Addendum List to the *National Register of Historic Places* and the *State Register of Historic Places* in

Wisconsin. Madison: State Historical Society of Wisconsin, 1998.

Archer, Marion Fuller. *Wisconsin: Forward!* Fenton, Mich.: McRoberts Publishing, 1978.

Austin, H. Russell. *The Wisconsin Story: The Building of a Vanguard State.* Milwaukee: The Milwaukee Journal, 1962.

Bell, Jeannette, and Chet Bell. *County Parks of Wisconsin.* Rev. ed. Black Earth, Wis.: Trails Books, 2000.

Bewer, Tim. *Acorn Guide to Northwest Wisconsin.* Madison: Prairie Oak Press, 1999.

Blake, William. *Cross and Flame in Wisconsin: The Story of Methodism in the Badger State.* Stevens Point, Wis.: Worzalla Publishing Company, 1973.

Brown, Dorothy Moulding. *Wisconsin Indian Place-Name Legends.* N.p.: Wisconsin Centennial Folklore, 1948.

Feldman, Michael, and Diana Cook. *Wisconsin Curiosities.* Guilford, Conn.: Globe Pequot, 2000.

Gard, Robert E., and L. G. Sorden. *The Romance of Wisconsin Place Names.* New York: October House, 1968.

———. *Wisconsin Lore: Antics and Anecdotes of Wisconsin People and Places.* New York: Duell, Sloan and Pearce, 1962.

Great Lakes Inter-Tribal Council. *Native Wisconsin: Official Guide to Native American Communities in Wisconsin.* Lac du Flambeau, Wis.: GLITC, 1998.

Grignon, David J. (Nahwahquah). *Menominee Tribal History, Commemorating the Wisconsin Sesquicentennial 1848–1998.* N.p.: Menominee Indian Tribe of Wisconsin, 1998.

Heritage Wisconsin: *Open a Treasure of African American Culture in America's Heartland.* Madison: Wisconsin Department of Tourism, 1998.

Hintz, Martin, and Dan Hintz. *Wisconsin Off The Beaten Path,* 4th ed. Guilford, Conn.: Globe Pequot, 1998.

Holliday, Diane Young, and Bobbie Malone. *Digging and Discovery: Wisconsin Archeology.* Madison: State Historical Society of Wisconsin, 1997.

Hunt, N. Jane, ed. *Brevet's Wisconsin Historic Markers and Sites.* Sioux Falls, S. Dak.: Brevet Press, 1974.

Leary, James P. *Wisconsin Folklore.* Madison: University of Wisconsin Press, 1998.

Marceil, Beauford, and Kathleen Marceil. *Stories of the Wisconsin Indians: Legends and Tales of She-She-Pe-Ko-Naw.* Self published, 1955.

March, Richard, and Marshall Cook. *Wisconsin Folklife: A Celebration of Wisconsin Traditions.* Madison: University of Wisconsin Press, 1998.

Normandin, Robert. *Catholic Travel Guide—Wisconsin.* St. Paul, Minn.: self published, 1995.

Official Wisconsin Travel Guide. Madison: Wisconsin Department of Tourism, 1999.

Olsenius, Richard, and Judy A. Zerby. *Wisconsin Travel Companion: A Unique Guide to the History Along Wisconsin's Highways.* Wayzata, Minn.: Bluestem Productions/Mijaz, Inc., 1983.

Preus, J. C. K., ed. *Norsemen Found a Church: An Old Heritage in a New Land.* Minneapolis: Augsburg Publishing House, 1953.

Rajer, Anton, and Christine Style. *Public Sculpture in Wisconsin.* Madison: SOS Wisconsin, Save Outdoor Sculpture and Fine Arts Conservancy Services, 1999.

Rummel, Reverend Leo. *History of the Catholic Church in Wisconsin.* Madison: Wisconsin State Council, Knights of Columbus, 1976.

Stone, Lisa, and Jim Zanzi. *Sacred Spaces and Other Places: A Guide to Grottos and Sculptural Environments in the Upper Midwest.* Chicago: School of the Art Institute of Chicago Press, 1993.

U.S. Department of the Interior. *Wisconsin Architecture: A Catalog of Buildings Represented in the Library of Congress,* by Richard W. E. Perrin. Historic American Buildings Survey. Washington, D.C.: 1965.

Visser, Kristin. *Frank Lloyd Wright and the Prairie School in Wisconsin: An Architectural Touring*

Guide. Madison: Prairie Oak Press, 1992.

Wisconsin Atlas and Gazetteer. 3rd ed. Freeport, Maine: DeLorme Mapping, 1998.

Wisconsin Auto Tours. Madison: Wisconsin Department of Tourism, 1992.

Wisconsin Cartographer's Guild. *Wisconsin's Past and Present: A Historical Atlas*. Madison: University of Wisconsin Press, 1998.

Wisconsin State Park Visitor Guide. Madison: Wisconsin Department of Tourism, 1999.

Woodward, David, and others. *Cultural Map of Wisconsin: A Cartographic Portrait of the State*. Madison: University of Wisconsin Press, 1996.

Wyatt, Barbara, project director. *Cultural Resource Management in Wisconsin: A Manual for Historic Properties*. Vol. 3. Madison: State Historical Society of Wisconsin, 1986.

Local Churches

Avella, Steven M. *Milwaukee Catholicism: Essays on Church and Community*. Milwaukee: Knights of Columbus, 1991.

Bittner, Bernadette Durben. *History of Churches in Sauk County, Wisconsin, Featuring "Ghost Churches."* Self published, 1977.

Braunschweig, Reverend. A. L. *St. James Lutheran Church, Verona, Wisconsin, 1886–1986*. Verona, Wis.: St. James Lutheran Church, 1986.

Breines, Reverend Andrew R. *Holy Redeemer Mission, Perry, Wisconsin, 1861–1961: A Case Study*. Madison: Craftsman Press Corp., 1961.

Brophy, Reverend Robert J. *Centennial Directory 1895–1995 of St. Ignatius Catholic Church*. N.p.: St. Ignatius Catholic Church, 1995.

Brophy, William K., ed. *Commemorative History of the Catholic Diocese of Madison 1946–1996: Building Our Future in Faith*. Madison: Roman Catholic Diocese of Madison, 1996.

Centennial Book Committee. *A Celebration of 100 Years of Parish Community: St. Joseph's Church 1884–1984*. N.p.: St. Joseph's Church, 1984.

Dewel, Robert C., comp. *The People Called Methodists: Baraboo, Wisconsin, 1840–1902*. Baraboo, Wis.: First United Methodist Church, 1992.

Engel, Dave. *Home Mission: A History of the First Congregational, United Church of Christ, Wisconsin Rapids, Wisconsin*. Rudolph, Wis.: River City Memoirs, 1987.

Erickson, Lorry Ann. *St. Anne's Hill—The Plain Shrine: A History of St. Anne's Hill, Plain, Wis.* Wilson, Wis.: SeS Publishing, 1996.

Gurda, John. *New World Odyssey: Annunciation Greek Orthodox Church and Frank Lloyd Wright*. Milwaukee: The Milwaukee Hellenic Community, 1986.

Hamilton, Mary Jane. *The Meeting House: First Unitarian Society, Madison Wisconsin*. Madison: Friends of the Meeting House, 1991.

Holand, Hjalmar R. *Coon Valley: An Historical Account of the Norwegian Congregations in Coon Valley*. La Crosse, Wis.: Litho-Graphics, 1976.

Manthe, Norbert M. *A History of Zion Evangelical Lutheran Church, Arlington, Wisconsin: 125 Years of God's Grace 1863–1988*. Arlington, Wis.: Zion Evangelical Lutheran Church, 1988.

Markevitch, Bernard J., and others. *Amazing Grace: A Sesquicentennial Remembrance, 1847–1997*. Sheboygan, Wis.: Gallimore and Zimmerman, 1997.

Minde fra Jubelfesterne paa Koshkonong (50th Anniversary of the First Koshkonong Lutheran Church). Decorah, Iowa: Den norsfe Synodes Bogtryfferi, 1894.

Nelson, E. Clifford, ed. *A Pioneer Churchman: J. W. C. Dietrichson in Wisconsin, 1844–1850*. New York: Twayne Publishers, 1973.

"On This Log, in 1944, Lutherdale Was Prayed into Being." *Lutherdale Log* (newsletter), 2000.

St. Francis Friary and Retreat Center: A Pilgrim's Guide to the Past and Present. Burlington, Wis.: St. Francis, 1979.

"St. Wenceslaus Church, Waterloo, Wisconsin." *Nase Rodina*—Newsletter of the Czechoslovak

Genealogical Society, no. 3 (1991), 67–68.

Urness, Jon, and Judy Urness. *Vermont Lutheran: 1856–1981*. Black Earth, Wis.: Vermont Lutheran Church, 1982.

Wagner, Reverend Harold Ezra. *The Episcopal Church in Wisconsin, 1847–1947: History of the Diocese of Milwaukee*. Milwaukee: Diocese of Milwaukee, 1947.

Other Local Resources

Adams County Wisconsin: A Graphic History. Friendship, Wis.: Adams County Historical Society, 1975.

Anderson, Harry H., and Frederick I. Wilson. *Milwaukee: At the Gathering of Waters*. Milwaukee: Milwaukee County Historical Society, 1981.

Coulee Pathways Heritage Tourism Project. *From the Ice-Age to the Interstate*. New Lisbon, Wis.: Coulee Pathways, 1999.

Dane County Hospital and Home Memorial. Verona, Wis.: Verona Public Library, 1993.

Eaton, Conan Bryant. "Rock Island: A Part of the History of Washington Township." *Door County Advocate*, 1969.

The Historic Perry Norwegian Settlement. Mt. Horeb, Wis.: Perry Historical Center, 1994.

A History of the Settlement of Darien, Allens Grove, and Fairfield. N.p.: Darien Bicentennial Committee, 1976.

Joseph, Frank. *Atlantis in Wisconsin: New Revelations about the Lost Sunken City*. St. Paul, Minn.: Galde Press, 1995.

Lange, Kenneth I., and Ralph T. Tuttle. *A Lake Where Spirits Dwell: A Human History of the Midwest's Most Popular Park*. Madison: Wisconsin Department of Natural Resources, 1975.

Link, Mike. *Journeys to Door County*. Bloomington, Minn.: Voyageur Press, 1985.

Markwardt, L. J. *The Blackhawk Country Club and Its Historic Indian Heritage*. Self-published, 1976.

The Marshfield Story, 1872–1997: Piecing Together Our Past. N.p.: Marshfield History Project, 1997.

The Northern Kettle Moraine State Forest Area. Campellsport, Wis.: Campbellsport Area Chamber of Commerce, 1999.

Paprock, John-Brian. *Guide to Spiritual and Religious Resources for South Central Wisconsin*. N.p.: Living Gold, 1997.

Peterson, Noble Paul E. *Tripoli Mosque*. Milwaukee: Tripoli Mosque, 1997.

Point of Beginnings: Heritage Trails of Southwest Wisconsin. Platteville, Wis.: Southwest Wisconsin Regional Planning Commission, 1999.

Reetz, Elaine. *Communities*, Vol. 1. *Come Back in Time*. Princeton, Wis.: Fox River Publishing Co., 1981.

Schultz, Helen A. *The Ancient Aztalan Story*. Lake Mills, Wis.: Aztalan Historical Society, 1969.

Skadden, Bill. *The Geology of Door County: A Self-Guided Tour*. Sturgeon Bay, Wis.: Golden Glow Publishing, 1978.

Effigy Mounds

Arntsen, Patricia A. *Prehistoric Geometrical-Based Art Work on the Ground: I. The Effigy Mound Region*. Madison: Ancient Earthworks Society, 1993.

Birmingham, Robert, and Leslie Eisenberg. *Indian Mounds of Wisconsin*. Madison: University of Wisconsin Press, 2000.

Birmingham, Robert, and Katherine Rankin. *Native American Mounds in Madison and Dane County*. Madison: State Historical Society and City of Madison, 1994.

Highsmith, Hugh. *The Mounds of Koshkonong and Rock River*. Ft. Atkinson, Wis.: Highsmith Press and Ft. Atkinson Historical Society, 1997.

Hurley, William M. *An Analysis of Effigy Mound Complexes in Wisconsin*. Anthropological Papers, no. 59. Ann Arbor: Museum of Anthropology, University of Michigan, 1975.

———. *The Wisconsin Effigy Mound Tradition.* Parts 1–2. Ann Arbor: University Microfilms, 1970.

Markwardt, L. J. *Black Hawk Indian Mounds on the National Register of Historic Places.* Self-published, 1979.

Rowe, Chandler W. *The Effigy Mound Culture of Wisconsin.* Westport, Conn.: Greenwood Press, 1956.

Wenzel, William, Patricia A. Arntsen, and James Scherz. *Survey Report Lizard Mound Park Washington Co., Wisconsin.* Madison: Ancient Earthworks Society, 1990.

More Great Titles

FROM TRAILS BOOKS AND PRAIRIE OAK PRESS

ACTIVITY GUIDES

Wisconsin Underground: A Guide to Caves, Mines and Tunnels in and Around the Badger State, *Doris Green*

Wisconsin's Outdoor Treasures: A Guide to 150 Natural Destinations, *Tim Bewer*

Acorn Guide to Northwest Wisconsin, *Tim Bewer*

Paddling Southern Wisconsin: 82 Great Trips by Canoe and Kayak, *Mike Svob*

Paddling Northern Wisconsin: 82 Great Trips by Canoe and Kayak, *Mike Svob*

Wisconsin Golf Getaways: A Guide to More Than 200 Great Courses and Fun Things to Do, *Jeff Mayers and Jerry Poling*

Great Cross-Country Ski Trails: Wisconsin, Minnesota, Michigan, and Ontario, *Wm. Chad McGrath*

Great Wisconsin Walks: 45 Strolls, Rambles, Hikes, and Treks, *Wm. Chad McGrath*

Great Minnesota Walks: 49 Strolls, Rambles, Hikes, and Treks, *Wm. Chad McGrath*

Best Wisconsin Bike Trips, *Phil Van Valkenberg*

TRAVEL GUIDES

The Great Wisconsin Touring Book: 30 Spectacular Auto Tours, *Gary Knowles*

Wisconsin Family Weekends: 20 Fun Trips for You and the Kids, *Susan Lampert Smith*

County Parks of Wisconsin, Revised Edition, *Jeannette and Chet Bell*

Up North Wisconsin: A Region for All Seasons, *Sharyn Alden*

Great Wisconsin Taverns: 101 Distinctive Badger Bars, *Dennis Boyer*

Great Wisconsin Restaurants, *Dennis Getto*

Great Weekend Adventures, *the Editors of Wisconsin Trails*

The Wisconsin Traveler's Companion: A Guide to Country Sights, *Jerry Apps and Julie Sutter-Blair*

Great Minnesota Weekend Adventures, *Beth Gauper*

Tastes of Minnesota: A Food Lover's Tour, *Donna Tabbert Long*

HISTORICAL GUIDES

Historical Wisconsin Getaways: Touring the Badger State's Past, *Sharyn Alden*

Walking Tours of Wisconsin's Historic Towns, *Lucy Rhodes, Elizabeth McBride and Anita Matcha*

Wisconsin: The Story of the Badger State, *Norman K. Risjord*

Barns of Wisconsin, *Jerry Apps*

Portrait of the Past: A Photographic Journey Through Wisconsin, 1865-1920, *Howard Mead, Jill Dean, and Susan Smith*

PHOTO BOOKS

Wisconsin Lighthouses: A Photographic and Historical Guide, *Ken and Barb Wardius*

Wisconsin Waterfalls, *Patrick Lisi*

The Spirit of Door County: A Photographic Essay, *Darryl R. Beers*

OTHER TITLES OF INTEREST

The Eagle's Voice: Tales Told by Indian Effigy Mounds, *Gary J. Maier*

The W-Files: True Reports of Wisconsin's Unexplained Phenomena, *Jay Rath*

The I-Files: True Reports of Unexplained Phenomena in Illinois, *Jay Rath*

The M-Files: True Reports of Minnesota's Unexplained Phenomena, *Jay Rath*

Northern Frights: A Supernatural Ecology of the Wisconsin Headwaters, *Dennis Boyer*

Driftless Spirits: Ghosts of Southwestern Wisconsin, *Dennis Boyer*

To place an order or for more information, phone, write or email us.

TRAILS BOOKS
P.O. Box 317, Black Earth, WI 53515
(800) 236-8088 • email: books@wistrails.com
www.trailsbooks.com